Working in
the Music Industry

Working in
the Music Industry

*A Guide to Careers in Commercial Music
and How to Get Those Jobs,
Including Interviews
with People in the Business*

Edgar M. Struble

Peter Panic Music

Please note that many of the interviews were conducted in the early 1990s. Salaries and hourly rates for various jobs in the music industry have risen since that time, and recording technology has progressed from analog to digital. Although such details have changed over the years, the interviewees' advice remains solid.

Contents

ACKNOWLEDGEMENTS

This project was initiated in 1989. Four children, a career change, two cross-country moves, and 20 years later, it was completed in 2009! When I started this project, Polla Cunningham listened to and transcribed many hours of taped interviews. So did Sandi Carney. My daughter Bethany transcribed the later interviews. My mother-in-law, Joan Lindroth, edited the first draft, and Sarah Jensen proofed and edited the final, both of them far better writers than I. Kelly and Michael Walker came up with a wonderful cover design and sage advice. The many people who graciously sat down with me and shared their expertise really made this book come alive, and I am deeply appreciative of their contribution. And through it all, my wife, Lauri, has been an unwavering source of inspiration and encouragement.

A special thanks to Bethany, Sarah, Hannah, and Rachel, and to God, who blessed me with these precious children.

<u>INTRODUCTION</u>

I made the decision to pursue music as a career when I was a high school senior. Like so many other musically inclined students, I had been playing dances, football pep rallies, and wedding receptions with small combos of two to six performers. There were two options after graduation: I could continue to play in local nightclubs or I could go to college, study music, and become an educator. I chose the latter.

Four years later I emerged from Michigan State University as a qualified band director with a degree in music education. The day I graduated I went on the road with a seven-piece rhythm and blues band. I never looked back nor have I ever taught music for a living, with the exception of substituting in the public school system one winter. I guess I always knew in my heart that I would be a performer of some sort (my grade point average in college certainly reflected this propensity). With reckless abandon, I set out to accomplish my goal. Those were lean years. Some weeks I got paid and some weeks I didn't, but it didn't matter. I was young, single, and, above all, I was doing what I loved to do most, playing music.

After a few years floundering around every nightclub in the Midwest, I set my sights a little higher and decided to seek my fame and fortune in Nashville. Kenny Rogers hired me in the fall of 1976 (more on that later). That was a turning point of sorts and I have been involved in the commercial music business on a national level since then.

I have discovered that there are many, many job opportunities in the music business that I didn't have an inkling of when I was a high school student in Scottville, Michigan. And that statement brings me to the purpose of this book. I suspect there are other people like me who want a career in the music business but do not have any idea what opportunities are available. Most high school students are told what I was: Go to college, get a degree, and become a music therapist, band director, choir director, or public school music teacher. The end. But it doesn't have to work that way.

We see performers on TV who are immensely successful. We buy their records, attend their concerts, buy their merchandise, and watch their videos. But what about the countless other people who make that success possible? Most of the public looks at an entertainer and never imagines the scope of the support team required to get that entertainer on the stage or to get an album produced or to get songs on the radio. Their roles are as diverse and multifaceted as the entertainment styles they support.

In the following pages I have tried to describe some of the career opportunities in the music business and have included interviews with people who are working in these occupations. Some of the people interviewed are giants in the industry; some are just starting out. Some work behind a desk and some work behind a drum set. Each story of how they got where they are is unique. You may be surprised to find that some of these people have few or no actual music skills, but their love of music combined with a willingness to work hard has led to their achievements in this alluring industry.

The music business is just that, a business, and its products are songs, albums, concerts, and merchandise. It requires product development and manufacturing, sales and advertising, lawyers and accountants just like any other industry. Figuring out how to best get the product sold is what makes any business go round. Every music industry job fits somewhere in that cycle. But I happen to think that unlike any other industry, the music industry is the most fascinating and rewarding.

So maybe you cannot play an instrument, but you love to read all the small print about studios, songs, or musicians that are included in the liner notes of a CD. Maybe you can't carry a tune in a bucket, but learning about behind-the-scenes people like managers and agents fascinates you. Maybe you are a musician but traveling is not your cup of tea. Be careful because you may be opening up more than just a book, you may be opening up a whole new world for yourself.

WORKING MUSICIANS

Road Musician, Recording Musician, & Symphonic Musician

The sounds of a jazz group drift to my room from the hotel courtyard where they are playing for guests at Sunday brunch. They sound very good. However, I suspect that some or all the musicians will go to another job Monday morning (their "day gig") and they won't pick up their instruments again until next weekend. You don't have to be a full-time musician to enjoy it. This section is for people who might want to pursue a full-time career in performance, but please do not discount part-time involvement in the music business. There is plenty of work for a "weekend warrior" and it's a good way to supplement one's income and have fun doing it.

For those who choose to be full-time musicians, whether in the studio or on the road, getting to that point can be the hardest part. You must have an unstoppable desire to "go for it." Patience and perseverance are required as well, for this is usually a process, not an event. I know of very few players who have simply walked into town and gotten a gig. More often than not, musicians end up taking a day job while this networking process evolves into the break that launches a career.

What if your break is a long time in coming? I am convinced that the place to look lies within. Are you really good enough? Do you have any alcohol or drug problems that are keeping you from success? How are your people skills? These are all questions that must be addressed before looking at any type of employment, but quite often are ignored by some musicians. I'll never forget the singer (quite good) I spoke with in a Holiday Inn lounge one night. Holding a double shot of tequila in one hand and a beer in the other he commented, "I don't understand it, I've been singing in these bars in Des Moines now for 23 years and I've never made it." By all means, be prepared to take a look at yourself and take the steps necessary to "clean up your act."

I only mention symphonic work briefly because I am focusing on the commercial music industry. However, I believe a career in classical music is viable for those with the interest and ability.

◯ *ROAD MUSICIAN*

When I was just getting started, I performed with a group that played at high school assemblies, pep rallies, and the dances after ball games that we called "sock hops." In college we played fraternity parties, dances, and anything else we could get. After college graduation, I went on the road with a rhythm and blues band and it seemed as if we played every bar in the Midwest. Then I moved to Nashville, and after four or five months of beating around in nightclubs, I was hired by Kenny Rogers to play keyboards in his road band.

The process can be essentially the same for anyone who wants to climb the ladder as a performing musician; however, the nightclub scene is not what it used to be. Many clubs are phasing out live music and replacing it with disc jockeys or automated systems. The exceptions are in the major music areas like New York, Los Angeles, and Nashville, where public demand and industry concerns have kept live music alive.

In Los Angeles, many clubs that feature live music charge the bands to play there and sometimes it's a stiff fee. The club owner charges the band a certain amount for the privilege of playing but allows the band to keep the cover charge. If the club gets a good crowd, the band might recover the fee paid to play and make some extra as well. However, if it's a slow night, the band could end up in the red. Talk about paying dues.

So where do you go if you want to play? There are still a few nightclubs that feature live music and there are always wedding receptions, private parties, and other "casual" gigs. A musician can make a modest living doing this type of work.

Getting hired as a road musician with a recording artist, as I did, is another possibility. You need to be located where that kind of music is going on – Los Angeles, Nashville, or New York City – because you can't afford to be two states away if there is an audition call. You have to be right there in the middle of it, meeting people, sitting in wherever and whenever you can, and getting to know the players who are already out there on the front lines. You need to get yourself in front of these people as often as possible and you need to be good.

Road musicians are generally paid by the day with rates that can vary greatly depending upon the income level of the artist/employer. Less established country acts pay approximately $100 to $200 a day. On the high end of the

2

scale, an established pop act might pay $500 to $1,500 a day. Some musicians are salaried on a yearly basis, but these situations are few and far between.

In January 1976, I moved to Nashville seeking fame and fortune. I met some musicians who were playing at a local Holiday Inn and sat in with them. I was invited back, and for about a month, I hung out at the Holiday Inn, sitting in and meeting people. I met many people who were in the music business in Nashville and through that networking effort I was able to get a job playing at the Ramada Inn six nights a week. Around that same time, Kenny Rogers started recording in Nashville and wanted to hire a Nashville-based touring band. He visited many of the clubs in Nashville, and ended up hiring my friends who were playing at the Holiday Inn. About five months later Kenny hired me as a third keyboard player on their recommendation.

My perseverance paid off. I was in the right place at the right time with the abilities and professional qualities needed to perform for a nationally known recording artist. Advancing to the position of musical director after two or three years, I stayed with Kenny for a total of 15 years. I kept that position because I enjoyed my work, I did my job well and was able to get along with my co-workers. I also continued to hone my abilities by keeping abreast of the technological changes in music and practicing as often as I could.

Interview with Tony King
Road Musician

Tony King hails from North Carolina and has worked both in country music and bluegrass. His first pro gig was with J.D. Crowe and the New South, where he served for three years as lead singer, lead/rhythm guitarist, and stage emcee. From there, he moved to Nashville to tour with Holly Dunn for two years and then with Vince Gill for two years as acoustic/electric guitarist and background singer. In 1992, Tony joined two other singers to form the trio Matthews, Wright and King. Signed to Columbia Records, the group recorded two albums and released five singles while touring as an opening act for Reba, Brooks and Dunn, and others.

Since then, Tony has toured with a host of top artists including Vern Gosdin, Chely Wright, Faith Hill, and Darryl Singletary and was a staff backup singer for two years for the popular Nashville Network show Prime Time Country. *He is currently in his 15th year of touring with legendary country duo Brooks and Dunn. His songwriting credits include cuts by Barbara Fairchild, Rhonda Vincent, Brooks and Dunn, and Ricky Van Shelton, who took Tony's song "I've Cried My Last Tear For You" to number one. Tony has also spent time in the studio, producing CDs for several gospel and bluegrass artists.*

Did you have any formal training in music?

Yeah, I got a bachelor's degree in music and vocal pedagogy from East Carolina University in Greenville, North Carolina.

Tell me about your transition from Greenville to Nashville and performing live.

Well, I was playing around in college – playing in bluegrass bands while I was studying opera. And that was really what I wanted to do, you know. I didn't really want to teach, and I didn't think I was quite good enough to get into the performance program, so the pedagogy program was somewhere in between. But really what I wanted to do was go out and play.

The last summer of my college years, I went to an audition with a bluegrass band and started working in Busch Gardens in Williamsburg, Virginia. So I did that for two summers, and one of the guys in the band lived in Tennessee, and he talked me into coming to Tennessee with him.

We started a bluegrass band around the Knoxville, Tennessee, area, and played at the '82 World's Fair. We were kind of the house bluegrass band at the Fair, and we played there six days a week for the whole six months of the '82 World's Fair.

I met a bunch of people that way, but I got frustrated at not really being able to make a living at it, so for some reason I ended up moving to Lakeland, Florida, for about a year, and I sold cars. During that time – I forget how – I had met J.D. Crowe. And out of the blue, I got a call from him. I guess people had told him about me while I was selling cars, so I got a call from him to audition. So I went up to Lexington, Kentucky, auditioned for the band, and got the job. And so from '83 to '86, I played with J. D. Crowe and the New South. And even though this was one of the biggest bluegrass bands in the country, we weren't making much money. I really couldn't make a complete living at it, so I worked part time with a termite company. (laughter)

This story gets better and better.

So I was playin' bluegrass on the weekends and killin' bugs during the week! (more laughter) And you know, I didn't like anything but bluegrass, but I got tired of crawling under houses and killing bugs so I started delving into country music. I bought an electric guitar and started working on that and ended up playing in a couple of local bands around Lexington in addition to playing with J.D. There was a lot of country music going on in Lexington in the mid-'80s, and a lot of the musicians ended up in Nashville with national acts.

I was out in California with J.D. and we were watching CMT, and I saw a video of a girl artist named Holly Dunn. And I thought, "She's pretty good. I wonder if she's got a band?" She was brand new at the time. So I called directory assistance for Nashville, Tennessee, and looked up Holly Dunn. And they gave me her number. (laughter) It was not unlisted, so I just called her out of the blue. I asked if she had a band, and as luck would have it, she was putting one together. So I sent her a record that I had done with J. D. where I was singing lead and playing lead guitar, and she hired me from that. So that's how I got to Nashville.

And you managed to stick around, right?

I played with Holly for two years, and near the end of that I got connected with Larry Strickland, who was married to Naomi Judd, and he was putting a vocal quartet together and wanted me to sing tenor. We were really close to a record deal with RCA. I remember getting ready to go down to the record label to work out the details of the contract, when Larry called to say the label had backed out. I had quit Holly to do this thing and it didn't pan out.

So for about a year I freelanced, but then I got hired by Vince Gill and worked with him for two years. Then Larry Strickland called again and asked if I would join up with Raymond Matthews and Woody Wright to form a recording trio. So we met each other, worked up a couple of songs, and a couple of days later we went in and sang for Steve Buckingham and some people at Columbia. And they signed us. (laughter)

Another amazing story!

Unfortunately, things didn't really pan out for the trio, but one thing that did pan out – we were opening for Brooks and Dunn, and when the trio came to an end towards the end of '93, I got a call from the Brooks and Dunn bandleader and he said they were looking for an acoustic guitar player and vocalist. I already had an offer to work with Reba, so I turned Brooks and Dunn down. The job with Reba never came through, so I was out of steady work for a few months. I did some fill-in work with Chely Wright, Vern Gosden, and Faith Hill. Then at the end of '94, Brooks and Dunn called back again, and I took the gig. I've been there ever since. In early 1996, my wife, Regina, and I got the *Prime Time Country* gig. (A Nashville Network daily variety show. –Ed.) So I was doing that TV show during the week and performing with Brooks and Dunn on the weekends.

What do you need to know in order to be a successful road musician?

I think you need to know how to ride a bus – and be around a bunch of people in close quarters. I've always said that you do the music part for free, but you get paid to ride the bus and be gone from home.

What would you tell someone just moving to town looking to do what you've done?

Don't do it. (laughter)

And then what would you tell them?

You know, a lot of people have asked me that, and I really don't know. The way I came in was pretty unusual. And it was back at a time when the whole music business was different. That's a tough one, because everyone I know has come to Nashville in a different way. They've gotten a job a different way. And most of it seems to be who you know. I've never gotten a job that I've done a cold audition for. Every job I've gotten has been by word of mouth. And for somebody who is just coming in – how to make people know who you are and what you can do, I don't know. I guess play in church, play in bars, and just make yourself as visible as you can. There are all sorts of small venues around town. You can walk in a club on lower Broadway and hear guys that will just blow your socks off the way they play – that are working for tips.

There's no formula for the rise to the top. I've seen guys come to town and get gigs 15 minutes after they've been here, and I've seen others that can be here for years without work. And there's probably a reason the guys that don't get work don't get work. Either they can't get along with somebody – too arrogant – or fold under the pressure of being in front of the crowd.

I guess if you come to town, just make yourself as visible as you can. Start a band. And a lot of it is the good ol' boy network. Somebody in town already has a job and they say, "Hey, I've got a friend that can do this." Go to auditions. The Union usually has notices about auditions. Go to clubs and listen around. Word gets around there about auditions and stuff. And the first part of the year, most people are looking to supplement their bands. The end of the year or the beginning of the next is when people, if they're going to make any changes, that's when it's going to happen. If people are going to make a change in their band, they'll give you the Nashville Christmas Present – a pink slip at Christmastime. (laughter)

What are some of the high points of your career?

I got to meet the President. And I've gotten to play the Grand Ole Opry a lot, which is a real cool thing. Working on that stage, if it doesn't affect you, you're just not breathing. We've gotten to open for some people I thought I'd never get to see, much less be with on the same show. Brooks and Dunn have opened for the Rolling Stones, we did a tour last year with ZZ Top. But just to be able to make a living in the music business period. It's not even like work sometimes.

Yes, you have to be away from your family a lot, and that is getting harder and harder.

And some of the low points?

We just found out two days ago that Brooks and Dunn aren't going to tour any more. I knew that would have to come to an end sometime. You've been there. You know how it is when you've done something for so many years. You just kind of back yourself into a corner as far as being able to do anything else. And the whole music business has turned into such a youth-oriented thing. Everybody that's hitting it big now seems to be covering a younger market. The chance of getting an equal job at my age – a parallel move is not looking too promising right now.

Given that Brooks and Dunn are calling it quits, what are some of your options? Are you looking to continue on as a road musician or would you like to pursue some other interests?

I would like to pursue other things, but that's what I mean about backing yourself into a corner. You do the road musician thing for so long that finding something else that you can do that will pay you that kind of money is tough. It's almost like starting over. I do have a possible option at church. They have called me about becoming a technical director. I've also been in the studio producing some gospel and bluegrass stuff. I'd like to do that as well. But I've made a lot of connections, so hopefully something will pop up.

⏻ RECORDING MUSICIAN

You have to be very, very good to be a recording musician. You also must be able to take direction well and be spontaneous, creative, and innovative for as many hours as you are in the studio – which can be a very long time. You need to know how to play many different styles of music and double on instruments related to the one you play. It is a very lucrative field. Good recording musicians earn about $75 to $100 an hour, usually in a three-hour time span known as a "session." Good studio musicians can work two or even three sessions a day and make $700 to $1,000 a day. The best command two or three times that.

Recording musicians usually start out by hanging around studios and playing on demo sessions (for next to nothing) whenever they get a chance. If you are a good player, eventually you will get calls for master recording sessions and television work.

You may be called upon to emulate certain sounds or styles that are in vogue at the time. This involves keeping your equipment as state-of-the-art as possible and bringing most of what you own to each recording session. If the producer wants a Stratocaster sound and all you brought is your Les Paul, don't be surprised if someone else gets the next recording session with that producer.

It is very hard to be a recording musician and a road musician at the same time. It not only involves two different styles of playing, but a successful studio musician must be there all the time. I seldom got calls to play on recording sessions during my years with Kenny Rogers because folks knew I was rarely in town.

Interview with Russ Cantor
Studio Musician

When one thinks of a studio musician, the picture of a guitarist, or perhaps a keyboardist usually comes to mind. However, there are many other types of instrumentalists who perform in the studio. One such player was Russ Cantor, a violinist who made his living as one of the "first call" studio musicians in Los Angeles. He certainly came up through the ranks, and had a good bit to say about how the process works. Since this interview was conducted, Russ has passed away.

What do you do?

As a freelance violinist, I am available for a wide range of calls. The studio calls, particularly the motion pictures, are the most favored. However, you can't always depend on just one thing. To be a successful freelance violinist you have to play in a number of different venues. So I will play, in an average season, everything from weddings to shows, record dates, TV series, motion pictures, sound tracks, jingles, and concerts. When you put all of those categories together you have a very interesting musical life. Not only is there variety of musical endeavors but a combination of different people, different chemistries that arise from all of these.

The most lucrative work is that which involves residuals. Motion pictures afford the most lucrative residuals. You get paid for the sessions that you record on, which could be anything from one single recording up to 10 days of double recordings. Almost invariably they release sound track albums. Then a year or two later, sometimes sooner, when the video cassettes come on the market, depending on how many they sell or rent, you get another piece of the pie on residuals. And it is perpetual. As long as it is being marketed you will continue to receive a percentage. There is a whole formula to determine what you are entitled to. If the product goes to network television, cable TV, or for foreign use, there are also additional monies.

With television, for the most part, you get paid for the amount of music or hours you record, period – it's over and out. Television work is not considered quite as desirable, but it is all good. If one industry is healthy, television versus motion pictures, one helps the other.

Speaking of that, I began freelancing back in '85 when I moved here from Las Vegas. Television was the primary studio employment. Now motion pictures are. It is not uncommon to see orchestras of 80 to 100 musicians recording a movie soundtrack with full string sections, full woodwinds, full brass, full rhythm, and exotic percussion instruments plus an entire synthesizer section. And this is largely due to composers such as John Williams, Jerry Goldsmith, James Horner, James Newton Howard, who are demanding these orchestras and unique sound palettes. It has been quite a turnabout from the austere days of the early- and mid-'80s when they were not using large orchestras.

Television, on the other hand, has diminished in its work opportunities. Most shows are using synthesizers or very small orchestras and the demand is much less. Thus one area goes down, but the other area goes up. It appears that records are making a comeback. The synthesized sound has gone full circle now. Everyone is used to the novelty of technology and it is now no longer so desirable to have this sound or do what this person or that act did. More and more you see a shift back to acoustic with one difference – you see a mix of electronics. We will never go back to just total acoustic instruments. There will always be a mix and I think that is the way it should be. This is my own personal feeling.

Synthesizers have wonderful resources – they can be awesome. Their technology may be used in an artistic manner to enhance the sound possibilities of music rather than as an economic way of displacing musicians. And that is starting to happen in motion pictures.

What is an average day for you when you are doing sessions?

The average day for me when I have sessions is fighting the freeway in the morning to get to MGM, Warner Bros., or Fox. You leave an hour and a half early to make your date. They begin at either 9:00 or 10:00; usually for motion pictures they are double sessions. You go to 5:00 or 6:00. There is actually six hours of recording on a double with a break for lunch of one hour.

Many times when we finish a date we'll go to the Music Center or some other venue for rehearsal with an orchestra to prepare for a weekend concert. It is very common to triple in respect to a session, one in the morning and one in the afternoon, and then the triple at night for the weekend concert. Some people will also do motion pictures at night when it's really busy.

What does it take to do what you do?

Well, all things being equal, you have to play. There is a certain quality and level that must be maintained. Although we can always suggest that we feel somebody doesn't deserve to be there, or we play better than this person, for the most part I would say that all the players are good.

Moreover, for studio work you have to be very sensitive to what is going on around you; you can't blast through with big sound and percussive attacks. You have to be conscious of blend, intonation, and rhythm. Of course we all use click tracks but even with click tracks, it means being accurate and playing very synchronized. It seems everything is exacerbated in the studio, because when the red light goes on it is so quiet you can hear a pin drop. You have to be very conscious of how much sound you are producing, what your vibrato and intonation are like. It's almost required you play antiseptically clean. Sometimes I find it frustrating because sometimes I feel I want to let go and be a little more emotional but you have to subject your own individuality for the whole. Principal players have a little more latitude, but they are still serving the composer or the situation.

There is very little room for the principal player to suggest that we try it another way. Once in a while the principal player will be justified in making a suggestion. It is always subjective to the composer's wishes.

What about personal qualities it takes to do this sort of work?

Politics is a very important ingredient in the studios. Most of the people that are successful in the studios are very proficient in social networking and politicking in the various areas that will enhance one's marketability. It's a given that you play well, but there are many people who play well that don't work in the studios. People like to feel comfortable with the people around them, so you want to market yourself in a way that enhances your likeability. People use each other on their respective jobs. In the music business, as in every business, we help those who help us.

What sort of background do you have that enables you to do this sort of work?

In my case, I began to study the violin at the age of 5. I studied with the finest teachers in Los Angeles. I was fortunate that I also had the opportunity to work commercially at a very young age. This created a very well-rounded musical perspective and gave me an important input musically that I don't think I would have had had I just remained a classical violinist. This perspective has helped me in the studio tremendously. I can understand classical, popular, commercial, jazz, and just about any other musical idiom. I feel the studio player in many respects is the most versatile player because he has to go from one idiom to another musically with equal facility in all.

What would you tell some young player who has a reasonable background, who is just getting off the bus from Des Moines, Iowa, to play and hopes to make it as a studio player? What advice would you have for him?

A young player coming to town with serious aspirations of playing the studios probably has already had serious achievements in their academic background. The studios are really comprised of the crème de la crème, those that could have gone on to a concert career, or a chamber music performance career, or joined the leading symphonies. So if a young person came to town I would assume they had those academic credentials. You have to be at a certain level to begin with. Necessary to get in to be a studio player is the new set of ingredients of networking, marketing, and getting people to know your product, to recommend you and put you on lists.

There are three ways of getting on lists: One is directly from the composer or arranger. If he/she asks for you or specifically makes a request to the contractor, almost invariably you will be hired. Second, have the contractor know your work and once again like you, and be recommended by other musicians, usually the principal players. Third are those principal players; they are sometimes asked by the contractors who they would like to have in their section. So for a young person, it would be important for them to go play for some of these people when they come to town and see how they fit in with this type of musical demand.

Is there an audition process one can go through?

Sometimes. I feel most of the auditions are done right in the trenches when you go out on a job. Usually within a few minutes someone says, "This person's doing good." Or it can go the other way: "This person's not cutting it," and they'll be weeded out. So there is a process, I guess like the NBA or NFL training camp, and you are being auditioned even though you're not auditioning. People that are already established in the business will be judging you and they will be spreading the word.

But there are young players, particularly some of the new Americans (those from other countries) who feel that the only way to get known is to audition for people. They will call up important musical figures, concertmasters, composers, or contractors and they will offer to go play for them directly. Some of that is successful some is not. Ultimately in the studios it is who will give your name. The more lists you are on and the more people that speak about you favorably enhances your work opportunities.

11

I do not want to mislead any young people. It is still not easy. You have to be very resilient and have a tough skin and be willing to take it on the chin for a long time. It may take many years to get established. It is not something that just happens. If someone needs money instantly they might be better to audition for a symphony or something that has a contracted period of employment. Working in the studios you have to be very patient and realize you are going to have periods where you make a great deal of money and periods where you make nothing.

I would also advise young people to listen to as many kinds of music as possible and to always use your brain as you are listening to it, getting pictures of sounds and styles in your mind. Not just reading notes, but how those notes fit in as a whole. The more versatile you can be the more valuable you are in the studio. And most important, keep up your performing skills – practice!!!

◊ *SYMPHONIC MUSICIAN*

This is one of the few jobs in the music industry that you can audition for and, if you are good enough, you can get the job. The key phrase is "good enough." However, you must be *more* than good enough to make a decent living playing in the symphonies – you must be among the best players in the country. The good news is, classical music has not yet been invaded by electronics. If you are a good cello player, some guy with an electronic keyboard and a drum machine will never take your job. The competition is fierce but there is still quite a bit of work in the major cities. Salaries range from $15,000 to $60,000 per year.

I recently learned about a young trumpet player who graduated from college and auditioned for the Los Angeles Symphony but didn't make it. He was told that there was an opening for the post horn player (the horn that "announces" events) at the racetrack in Long Beach. He went to Long Beach for the audition (which was just as tough as the symphony audition!) and got the job. He was able to play his horn every day, earn good money, and have enough free time to practice for the next round of auditions at the symphony. It beats digging ditches.

The military is another option for symphonic players. They hire all sorts of musicians and provide excellent training, decent pay and good benefits. I grew up with Marty Erickson who has been the principal tuba player for the United States Navy Band for several years. Besides being one of the best tuba players on the face of the earth, Marty does recording work in Washington, D.C. and plays some casuals on the side. He is like a regular symphony player except the members of his band wear uniforms instead of tuxedos. It's worth considering.

Interview with John Lawless
Timpanist with Chattanooga Symphony & Opera Association

What do you do?

I live in Atlanta and freelance, doing about half of the season with the Atlanta Symphony. I play the entire season of the Atlanta Opera, a lot of Broadway shows that come through like *The Phantom of the Opera*, and I'm also the timpanist with the Chattanooga (Tenn.) Symphony. Our percussion trio has been around for eight years and we do a minimum of 300 schools per year, generally two shows per school throughout the school year. I teach at two colleges: West Georgia as Head of Percussion and Georgia State University as the Timpani/ Latin Percussion Specialist. I have about 15 students in all between both schools. I also am a percussion coach for the Atlanta Symphony Youth Orchestra. I just completed a drum corps camp affiliated with the Spirit of Atlanta with kids from all over the South. That is a real interest for me, but you can't make money at that. I used to imagine that I'd be with a big orchestra, and I've auditioned around, but I'm quite happy with the diversity that my career allows now. Of course that means there is no steady paycheck; that is the drawback.

What is your background?

I started studying seriously when I was in seventh grade, working with a percussionist from the Atlanta Symphony. I went through the regional and all-state programs. I played with the Atlanta Symphony Youth Orchestra. I marched in a drum and bugle corp and played snare drum. I got a bachelor's degree from Georgia State. I never pursued a higher degree because I was working so much. The only thing that I thought I would lose out on was teaching college and the two colleges approached me anyway based on merit and not on a degree basis.

It has always been my contention, in the symphonic field anyway, that if you can go and play the audition and you're good enough, you'll get hired. What is your reaction to that?

It is the most frightening thing, and an extremely unfair way to assess someone's ability. I know a lot of people that can audition wonderfully but cannot play in an orchestra. But what else can they do?

I just played an audition in San Antonio, even though it would have been a cut in pay. I got to see a lot of guys I hadn't seen in a while. They listened to timpanists for 12 hours and took eight of those players for another round. We played the 13th hour and they did not take anyone from our group even though we all felt we had played very well. But after 13 hours how could they even know what they were hearing anymore?

What about someone just starting out?

Get with a program that you want to pursue. There are so many different schools like Allen Able School in Philadelphia, a percussion and timpani school in Cleveland, in Los Angeles – Barry Jakowski and San Francisco Symphony, Sal Goodman School, Eastman and so on. Every one is different. Figure out what course you want to go and assess who is winning what jobs. If three or four Eastman, people have come out and won jobs, go to Eastman. Then lock in with a good teacher like a Corey Duff, or a John Beckett at Eastman, or any of the big names.

Allen Able is sending out some incredible percussionists now and he gets people into auditions. If you are in good with the teacher and he likes what you do, they can help you a lot. They know when an audition is coming up. They know when someone is retiring maybe a year before it happens and they can hone a student right into that spot.

Now it is so competitive. I have been close sometimes and it is not because of nerves. If you miss one note you're out. The audition panel is looking for a way to delete names. You put out several hundred dollars to get to the audition and practice for months and then blow it in a blink of an eye.

I got a call in Atlanta that Chattanooga needed a timpanist. I came and played a solo audition that lasted about an hour and the maestro said that was exactly what he had in mind and I was hired on the spot.

Do you think you'll be able to go full time with the Atlanta Symphony?

Again, that will be a full-scale national audition. There is a good chance I'll make the finals just because I have been playing with them for some time, but you're still in the free-for-all. The Atlanta Symphony is becoming quite prestigious and is moving ahead quite rapidly. The pay scale is also very attractive at about $50,000 a year with eight weeks off a year. Consequently, there will be a lot of players wanting to get in.

What advice do you have for someone coming out of high school who wants to be in an orchestra?

Don't close the door by saying that you only want to be an orchestral player. There are too many things that you can do. As soon as you go to your first audition you'll see 75 people that play as well as or better than you. And you thought that they'd hear you and hire you right away. It's really a miracle to get a job right out of school. You really have to pay your dues. Don't have blinders on; do other things. Find groups to play with. There is so much out there that is exciting.

<u>COMPOSERS</u>

Songwriters, Film Scoring, Jingle Writers,
Arrangers, and Copyists

Composers are often thought of as Beethoven-like people who write symphonic scores for orchestras. Composers in commercial music are the songwriters, film scorers, and jingle writers. Arrangers and copyists also play an important role in the process. This section takes a look at each of these categories and some of the people who are active in these fields. Any resemblance to Beethoven is purely coincidental.

SONGWRITER

What does it take to be a songwriter? Songwriters are a mysterious blend of talent, expertise, practical knowledge, and the uncanny ability to touch the public's heart. The best songwriters, like all good musicians, practice what they do day after day. In fact, some of the best tunes are co-written. Many successful writers work with someone with whom they have good "chemistry," like Hal David and Burt Bacharach. A songwriter does not have to be a virtuoso on any instrument but *does* have to come up with music and/or words that say something and affect people.

The ability to write poetry does not make a person a songwriter. Many tunes are sent to me that amount to nothing but poems set to music. There are words and rhymes that are fine in poetry but would make people laugh if they were used in the context of a popular song. Also, there are some very good musicians who are lousy songwriters. It takes a special talent to begin with and the persistence to develop that talent. I have been in this business 40 years and when I came to Nashville in 1976 I thought I was a songwriter. I thought I was going to take the town by storm. I found out very quickly that (even though I was a good musician) I was not a good songwriter. It took me another 10 years

16

or so before I wrote anything commercially acceptable, and I'm still working toward a "hit."

I would advise anyone who wants to get started as a songwriter to first find a place where there is a creative environment. Nowadays, that could be online, but I really advise a move to a town where there are other songwriters and you can actually get to know some of them. You can meet them at "writer's nights" at various nightclubs or by hanging around recording studios.

Try to co-write with some of the people you meet. Every major music city has a songwriter's organization that may be helpful both in improving your skills and in marketing your tunes. It may take a couple of years before anyone will take you seriously, but if your songs speak for themselves, the doors will start to open. Perhaps a small publisher will be willing to work with you on a song-by-song basis. Above all, keep your ears and eyes open, listening for new ideas and new inspiration.

Eventually if you are good enough, a publishing company may hire you as a staff writer. In addition, if you hang out in a music town long enough, you're bound to meet some of the folks who are actually making records. As in most of the music business, it's all about relationships and networking.

Interview with Frank Myers
Songwriter

Frank J. Myers is from Dayton, Ohio. Shortly after moving to Nashville in 1981, he became bandleader, road manager, and lead guitarist for country star Eddy Raven. It was with Eddy that Frank started writing, playing, and co-producing sessions, resulting in two No. 1's, five No. 2's, and three in the Top 10. Their songs include "I Got Mexico," "Bayou Boys," "You Should've Been Gone By Now," "Sometimes a Lady," and many others. Frank's first single was one he wrote himself, 1982's "You and I" for Eddie Rabbitt and Crystal Gayle. The song was a crossover hit in country, pop, and adult contemporary.

During his time with Eddy Raven, Frank met Gary Baker. They had their first No. 1 together in 1993 with "Once Upon a Lifetime" by Alabama. Gary and Frank recorded one album for MCG/Curb Records and were three-time nominees for Duo Of The Year at the ACMs and CMAs. Their greatest accomplishment as writers together came when John Michael Montgomery recorded "I Swear," which was No. 1 for four weeks on the country charts. The song was then recorded by All 4 One and went to No. 1 on the pop charts where it stayed for 11 weeks, winning many writing awards.

17

Frank continues to write prolifically. He wrote the latest single for country artist Bucky Covington, "I Want My Life Back" and new artist Ash Bowers' single "Stuck." He is currently producing and writing for new country artist Matt Gary.

What do you do as a songwriter?

I go in every day and try to write songs, or every other day. I'm always looking for themes and titles that you can sink your teeth into. When you have a great idea it's easier to write a great song. In essence, a song is a three- or four-minute short story. Then melodically, I just try to marry the melody and feel with that lyric. I think when all those combinations come together and you can connect with the listener's own life or fantasies, that's when you have a hit on your hands.

Where did you learn how to do this?

Well, I think first of all you have to have a God-given ability to do it and then you just develop the craft after that. Also, I've learned a lot through the years from different people.

Eddy Raven was of course my first influence and I've learned from other writers, like Don Pfrimmer, who is strictly a lyricist. And then musically, I grew up in a musical family. I've been playing guitar since I was 9. And I've played all sorts of different kinds of music so I have a lot of different musical influences back in the library.

So when did you actually get started writing? And after you realized you were a songwriter, how long did it take for you to get something that was a measurable success?

I don't know if I've ever sat down and said I'm a songwriter. But when I lived in Ohio, I started putting music to lyrics. My sister had written some lyrics that I put some music to and I did some with a vocal instructor. I moved to Nashville in April of '81, started working with Eddy (Raven) in June or July '81, and immediately, I'd say by fall, we were starting to write together. And I mean, it happened fast because I moved here in April '81, and then September of '82, that's when "You and I" came out, which I wrote by myself. That was a huge hit for Eddie Rabbitt and Crystal Gayle.

That's actually amazing. I don't think it happens that quickly for most.

No it doesn't, and I was just very fortunate and blessed that it did happen like that.

Did you attract any publishers when you first came to Nashville?

Well, I think you have the God-given talent and then He expects you to work hard. God helps those who help themselves. But I've been very blessed. Without Him in my life, probably none of it would have happened. You know, that's what I think. Everything comes from Him; the ideas, the inspirations, everything. Obviously you have to work hard, and be persistent, and have that faith that everything's going to work out. Put everything in His hands, because you have down times. The music business, as you know, is very up and down.

When you're writing, what does and average day look like for you?

Well, it varies. The majority of the time I start by 10:30 or 11, and I'm finished by 3 or 4 o'clock.

You actually set aside that portion of the day to write with someone or by yourself. This is something that doesn't just happen, right?

Most of the time it's appointments that are set up, and you meet and you write. Hopefully, you'll have something to write about.

And how often during the course of a week will you do that?

Sometimes every day. Sometimes three times a week. It varies depending on the time of year. I work a little bit harder between August and March, April. I hit May, June, and July and sometimes it's not as frantic. There's really no set thing. You can work as hard or as little as you want to.

Did you attract any publishers when you first came to Nashville?

I guess not when I first came. Obviously when we did "You and I." Eddie Rabbitt's publishing company got that.

What would you tell somebody who is starting out as a writer today?

I'd tell them to read and search for ideas and stories. And to write every day. And to write with people who are better than they are, and learn.

How do you network with other songwriters if you're new in town?

Join organizations like NSAI – that's the Nashville Songwriter's Association International. Great organization. And there they can meet other new songwriters and collaborate. And they should to go to the Bluebird (The Bluebird Café – a famous Nashville songwriter's hangout) and different places and try to get on some writers nights. That sort of thing. You know, networking is a big thing no matter what you're doing.

How has the business changed within the last few years with regard to writing and the economics of things?

Well, we're obviously losing a lot of money and losing a lot of writers by people stealing the music. Illegally copying it and downloading it, that takes the money out of our pockets. Some writers, they may only have one hit record, and if people don't pay for it, you know, it's hard to survive. But you know, I think things are coming around some on that. It would be really simple if the government would just step in and make Internet service providers, make these sites collect the money. Or shut down the peer-to-peer sites that are letting people do this. It's really easily remedied, in my opinion. It's a government thing. And AOL, Comcast, or whoever it is, it's the Internet provider who knows what's going on.

◊ *FILM COMPOSER*

Film scoring is the process of creating music for films. A film composer has to be familiar with film editing and recording techniques. He/she needs an understanding of what is called critical timing, i.e., when certain actions or motions take place on screen, the musical notes or accents fall in place with the action.

Most film composers are one-person operations. The digital revolution has allowed composers to work from their home studios from start to finish on a film or TV scoring project. Composers of feature film scores still use large orchestras to record their scores, but usually a digital mock-up is made so the director can approve the music before it is actually recorded by the orchestra. A major film composer may also enlist the help of an orchestrator and a music copyist to get the score ready for a recording session.

I think the most important thing a film composer does is to create a mood. Good music has often saved a bad motion picture.

How do you become a film composer? You can go to school for it. Although there are some "seat of the pants" film composers who are doing very well (Danny Elfman for example), most successful writers have had some formal training.

There are schools on the West Coast that specialize in film scoring and some community colleges have film classes that allow students to become familiar with part of the process. You can get to know people taking acting or directing classes and perhaps get to score one of the student films.

There is very good money for composers who get movie or TV work. Six figure incomes are common. Scoring low-budget films, training videos, corporate videos, or local TV spots can yield a living wage. However, there is a lot of competition, and as a result, composing budgets have gone down over the last 20 years or so.

The usage of library music has dramatically increased, especially in TV work, and that has further eroded the amount of work that is available to composers. There is the option, however, of creating music for these music libraries. I find it to be a good source of supplemental income, and for some it can be a primary source of revenue.

Interview with Larry Brown
Film/TV Composer

I could have interviewed Larry for any one of several categories. He is an Emmy-winning engineer and a successful producer, has toured with national acts, and has been a first-call studio drummer in L.A. As a TV/film composer, Larry has the ability to create, perform, and record his work, all from the comfort of a digital studio in his house!

What are some of the film and television projects you have worked on?

The movie *Blind Date, Kenny Rogers Classic Weekend* for three years, *Quiz Kids Challenge*, a lot of animation stuff by Murakami-Wolf-Swenson, cartoon shows like *Pretty Piggies, Toxic Crusaders, James Bond Jr., Barnyard Commandos*, and a weekly sci-fi drama called *War of the Worlds*. I started doing scoring themes for American International Pictures: *Wild Angels* – an early biker picture.

How did you get this work to begin with?

I had been working as a musician and as an engineer. I had been engineering on films like this already so I knew what was going down on them. One day I was asked to work on a film as composer, I said yes, and that led to more pictures.

What do you have to know to do what you do?

A good understanding of film and television principles, dealing with budgets, dealing with timings, and a good sense for scoring action on screen, which is actually the easiest part. As far as training or education is concerned, a person with a strong musical background and a good sense for mixing audio and visuals together can probably score. This includes having the hands-on experience as a player and a working knowledge of the technical aspects of scoring.

If you were just starting out in this business, knowing what you know now, what steps would you take to become a film composer?

I would definitely study composition, although I don't think that is the most important thing. I think the biggest thing is you have to have that inbred sense of musically what is right, and you have to be a good enough player to pull it off.

Now we are dealing with a new age of composing where a lot of stuff is done not strictly with a big orchestra. We can do a lot of stuff on computer, whereas 15 years ago when I started we had to use a band. I'm not saying that one should not use a band. It is always my first choice, but (especially dealing in television, which is mostly what I have done) scoring on computer can be done in less time and more cost effectively. (I would also say that studying these new technologies is very important.)

Is scoring for television any different from movies?

Basically not. It's just that you have less time and less money. You are still trying to make your music work with something visual on a screen. The biggest difference is that you have better visual material in films than you do with television, so you have to work a little harder maybe in TV. Also for the arrangements in TV, you don't have to think quite as big as you do in film. You can get away with a bit less orchestration. You don't want to overplay your action on-screen, which is always a good rule of thumb anyway. I find most film writers can write for TV and most TV writers can write for film. However, film writers don't want to write for TV because they are used to the bigger budgets and the additional work time that they have with film projects.

What about the use of home MIDI* studios as opposed to using live musicians?

I operate out of a home studio. It depends a lot on the film. I do a lot of computer stuff but I also use live players mixed in with that. When I say computers, I'm not implying that the music is created by a computer. Everything that goes on the computer is played by a live player (which in my case I play myself). In many cases, composers bring in a keyboard player.

Still, a musician is playing the part, so it's not like some soulless piece of music sitting on a hard drive somewhere. Somebody has breathed life into it. I don't look down on it at all.

However, there's something special that you get when a group of musicians gather in a room, a kind of magic. There is the interplay between musicians that you don't get when one person plays all the parts. Of course, there's also that sonic tradeoff; there is something very stirring about putting 30 to 40 guys in a room and having all that air move around in there. You just don't get that from a computer.

But if you are dealing with television in a small speaker, that doesn't always translate anyway, so it's not that much of a big deal. Dealing with film on a large screen where everything is somewhat bigger than life in front of you, I think it becomes more important to deal with a live band.

* MIDI – Musical Instrument Digital Interface

Did you study music when you were young?

As a kid I grew up taking classical piano lessons from age 7 to about age 16 and did the whole bit with recitals, etc. I was in orchestra, band, and marching band all through high school. I was involved with anything that had to do with music. I was a music major in college. I left college to go on the road as a musician, then went back again to study composition. I also studied computers at a private music school, Dick Grove's School of Music, when it first opened up. This is where I got my first taste working with computers and electronic keyboard stuff. The rest of it was the school of hard knocks.

How much can a film composer expect to make?

That, of course, depends on how good you are and how much work you get. A person doing a small budget film maybe has a $20–25,000 music budget. Somebody doing two to three features a year and maybe a TV show could be making up to $750,000 to $1,000,000 a year. People who are doing multiple TV series (like Mike Post) are pulling in multi-million figures per year. These are people who have been doing this for many years and are seeing residuals off television, which is really one of the nice perks in the business. With the residual system, you get paid every time the show is played. (Payment is made by a performance rights society – in this country, BMI, ASCAP or SESAC. Payment rates are calculated by each society as a result of their monitoring air use of their writers' and publishers' works. –Ed.)

You are paid by the minute of music. The rate depends on whether it is a network show and the time of day the show runs. It is quite profitable. The average show will pay roughly 33 cents per minute for music. You get paid per market, per play, per minute. A good live action adventure weekly television show might have 18 to 30 minutes of music in it. Take that times 33 cents times 150 markets or stations times 52 weeks. Then you can figure the kind of money you can expect to make per year. (This amounts to $46,000 to $77,000 per year. –Ed.) Multiply that by 33 cents by 150 markets or stations by 52 weeks to figure what you can expect to make per year.

23

Film is a whole different ballpark. At the moment, there is no pay to the composer for theater play of a composition (in the United States). You get paid for theatrical play of compositions in Europe only, and that takes you quite a few years to see. That is part of why film budgets are quite a bit larger than television budgets. You make it up front in film and on the back end in television.

Television is probably the more lucrative of the two, even though there is a lot more pressure. Also aesthetically it is not quite as pleasing because you are working under much tighter schedules and much smaller budgets.

○ *JINGLE WRITER*

A jingle writer is a songwriter who uses his or her talent to promote a product. One of the more famous jingle writers is Barry Manilow who wrote commercials for McDonalds and Coca-Cola before he achieved fame as a pop singer.

It is helpful for the jingle writer to be familiar with the advertising business and marketing techniques. These skills can be learned in college or as an apprentice with an advertising agency. This is a very competitive field and the top performers can make incredible amounts of money. The average jingle writer in a regional market can make a respectable living.

One doesn't just fall into this business. Success at a national level is obtained usually after a lengthy period of floundering around in local, then regional markets. And, like so many other businesses, individual performance determines your level of success.

Local radio stations are good places to start. If you have some songwriting or instrumental skills, it is possible to utilize them in the advertising department of a local station. If you're good enough, possibly you'll attract the attention of an advertising agency or a bigger radio station. If you continue to perform well, perhaps someday you'll be cranking out enough fast food ads to keep you in French fries the rest of your life!

Each trade has its tools, and the jingle business is no exception. A small home studio is a big plus, as it enables the composer to create demos, or in some cases, complete jingles at a reasonable price. With each piece you write, you can add another example of your work to your demo reel. That and a brief resume are helpful in securing work from agencies who otherwise might not be aware of your talents. Be advised however, that large ad agencies get hundred of reels from aspiring jingle writers and that submitting a tape is effective only if you've done the networking required to get it listened to.

Interview with Dan Williams
Jingle Writer

Retired, but at the time of this interview, the head of one of the best jingle houses in America, Dan Williams came to Nashville as an aspiring songwriter in 1970. In 1983 he co-wrote the No. 1 country hit for Ronnie Milsap, "Don't You Know How Much I Love You." Most of the songs he writes now are for 30- or 60-second jingles. "It's kind of like, a verse and a chorus and you're home," Williams says. "Of course, it has to be a good verse and chorus."

How did you get started?

I was in a band that won an East Texas battle of the band competition and some free studio time was given to us. We had to have something to record so I wrote a song. The guy at the studio liked it and for the next couple of years, age 16 to 18, I wrote 90 to 100 songs. I was a pop/rock and roll songwriter, and just as I turned 19, I moved to Nashville.

I had a lot of trouble because no one wanted to listen to me except this one guy who gave me the opportunity to write some jingles. I didn't really even know what he was talking about. The first one that I did was for Busch Beer, so I started nationally which is very unusual. They were actually 60-second songs instead of a hard-sell commercial.

I really haven't drifted from that concept much at all in the 21 years that I have been doing this. As the jingles were put on the air, the stations started getting many phone calls about them and requests to play those commercials. I liked that sort of writing and actually got paid for it, so that's how I got started. I moved back to Texas a couple of years later.

Even after my initial success, I still wanted to do the songs, not jingles. I hadn't grown up yet. In 1978, I moved back to Nashville and decided I really wanted to get into it. The first spot that I wrote was for Red Lobster and that was "The Seafood Lover in You," which is still running.

What does it take to be a successful jingle writer?

Maybe a little bit of uniqueness, originality. Maybe it's because I grew up as a songwriter. I didn't grow up writing jingles. I'm not really into the jingles, per se. This company likes to put a record approach to what we do and I think that is what makes us different. We put a little more heart and soul in our stuff. Everybody likes to say that, but I really believe that.

When you were trying to get your stuff noticed by people, how did you go about that?

When I started in 1978, I was with a group of six or seven guys writing with a house in Nashville, which was in competition with several other music houses. You just have to put your work in there and hopefully it wins. From 1978 into the early 1980s I won most of the stuff and I can't tell you why. I just work very hard at it. I think you just have to listen and try to stay abreast and ahead a little bit.

Did you have formal training?

Listening to the radio. That is how I learned to write songs.

As an established music house, do you offer any opportunities for apprenticeship?

Yes, there are many opportunities in the jingle business. I do most of the jingle writing here but in the industry there are many positions available for sales people, musicians, singers, and arrangers. You just have to be very focused.

What would you tell someone who is just getting started?

It is hard. The hard thing is punching in. To break into the jingle business I think you need to take a record approach to it if you want to get into the top echelon. Approach it as if you are writing 30- or 60-second songs. Also play your stuff to your friends, play it to everybody, and be very critical of yourself because you can really hurt yourself by bringing something in that is not good. Many times you only get one shot, so make the best of it even if it takes a little bit longer.

Do the jingle houses listen to unsolicited material?

Oh, yes. We try to listen to everything that comes in because you never know when you're going to find something. It's hard but not impossible.

Interview with Chuck Surack
Owner of Sweetwater, Fort Wayne, Ind.

Sweetwater is arguably the world's largest online music retailer. Chuck Surack started the business in 1977, working out of his garage, and the rest is history.

I was asked to call between 8 and 9 a.m. for the interview. That's because most musicians aren't out of bed yet, and Chuck would have time to talk. Around 10 o'clock the phones light up with calls from all over the country: orders to fill, service work to be performed, advice and instruction to be given. The studio is backed up with advertising clients and work continues into the night. It's a music metropolis right here in Fort Wayne – and it all started with a four-track Teac and a bunch of talent.

How did you get started?

Right in high school I played a lot of wedding bands, gig bands, and the like. The bands I was in never had vocals. We had a saxophone and trumpet player and played all the standards. I eventually went on the road as a musician playing full time in the typical Holiday Inn, Rodeway Inn type of band. I never had any very formal training other than in high school. My last year of high school I took just about all music related courses. I even did some teaching – electronic things and the like. I've always been into that. Most people didn't know it was a music-oriented school. I guess it really wasn't, but because I was at the top of my class I got to take charge of my curriculum. I studied anything that I could get my hands on related to music.

Anyway, I played on the road for several years and got to the point where being on the road was not exactly what I wanted to do long term. So I came home and thought I was going to get a real job. That lasted about three months. Then I slowly started getting back into music.

Being on the road for several years, I was going into recording studios with the bands that I was with. We'd go in to record, and come to find out, production came naturally for me, and I could make it sound better than the technical recording engineer. Quite often we'd record at small radio stations that had four or eight tracks so I'd end up being in charge on the recording session.

I had a natural inkling for the stuff and started piecing together my own equipment. I bought a four-track Teac and thought that was the be-all and end-all. I thought, boy, that's all I'll ever need, and I could do whatever I wanted to do with four tracks. It didn't take long to outgrow that technology so I went to eight-, 16-, 24-track, and now we're even looking at digital.

Now I had all this recording equipment and for the first several years I was recording bands and all sorts of people out of the living room of a mobile home. That was our recording studio. We had decent equipment and wrote pretty good stuff, but the bottom line was the music. Things that were coming out were sounding good. It's been an uphill battle from there, but I've developed a good business from those beginnings.

Did you have any success with that music early on?

Locally, yes. All the radio stations were playing stuff that came out of our studio. Then we got into the eight-track days and we had a local band that had songs on HBO, Cinemax, and Showtime. This was pre-MTV. The band was called Mark Urgent and the song was called "On a Night Like This." HBO played the song in regular rotation in between their feature movies for six weeks. In the meantime we were doing these bands at night. The bands were fun and all that, but it was hard to make money so we went after more corporate kind of stuff.

I can remember the first corporate thing I did. I was hired by a local audio/visual company to go to Ohio to the General Motors plant to record a year-end corporate speech. The only thing is, and this really put me on the map, the guy forgot what year it was. We finished with this hour-long tape for which the company is paying big bucks (this is a year-end presentation to the employees), and throughout the program the president of the company has given the wrong year. So for about six hours I got out razor blade and tape, copied and spliced and physically made the company president say the right year. I found somewhere else in his speech the consonant that I needed, copied it several times and spliced it in and the guy had a perfect speech. From that point on the company, AGS&R, (they are a very big slide show producer) is one of our biggest customers.

Explain a little bit about what you do now.

From a music production point of view, our biggest thrust is doing jingles, although we don't like to call them jingles, just music that you pay for. I don't care whether it's a jingle for radio, or for TV, or for background sound effects, or for video production. We do a lot of work for training films where they have us record a narration and then we post-score music around it – anything that is involved with music or the production of sound. We are doing everything from local jingles to national jingles to animated robots that teach kids about drugs, etc.

What is the key to your longevity in this business?

We are in Fort Wayne with about 200,000 people, maybe a million in the rest of the county. During the past 10-12 years that I have been here eight to 10 serious studios have come and gone. We make sure that what we do is right. I won't compromise to the point that if necessary, we'll work all night fixing the project to meet an eight o'clock deadline. We always do it right. There is only one way to do things and if it pays off, they (the clients) come back.

What about jingle writing? Are you involved in the creative end of that?

In the early days I did it all myself, and the last couple of years we've hired people to help.

What do you have that other people don't have that allows you to make successful commercials?

I don't know that there is anything specific; it's a combination of things. One thing that most people don't realize is plain, good old business techniques. Music is important, but to be honest it's just a small part in the total formula. I think anybody could write music and record it. It's getting along with people, being out there making contacts, being out there in the world that makes the difference. So much of our business is strictly from past reputation, referrals, people we know, that sort of thing.

You almost have to be a psychologist, balancing the creative people with the advertising people, who are ultimately working for a client, who is ultimately trying to sell the end customer. There are times that you feel in your gut that it should be this way and the client wants it that way.

At times you may feel as if you are selling your soul. I never thought that, however. I love the jingle business. Every day we are working on a different style of music, country to rock to big band to classical. I couldn't do that if I was a typical music producer doing rock albums or country albums or whatever. We've done thousands of 30- and 60-second pieces of music, every different kind imaginable.

What are your biggest accounts right now?

HWI, Super Iron Out, McDonalds, and Xerox.

How did you land national accounts out of Fort Wayne, which is not exactly known as a jingle town?

Connections. We work very hard to get referrals from our local agencies and past clients. There are a couple of agencies right here in Fort Wayne that just will not record with us. They think the "experts" are 500 miles away even though we do work for McDonalds, HWI, and other national accounts. They record everything in Indianapolis, yet I can't tell you how much we do for Indianapolis agencies. It gets to be funny after a while.

Have you ever advertised?

We do very little advertising. It's real hard to get the attention of the guys who write the ads at advertising agencies. Also, they get bombarded with hundreds and hundreds of tapes from musicians who think they can write jingles. If you go into any advertising agency I bet you they will have 20, 30, 40 tapes on the desk or on the wall from songwriters that think they can write jingles. It is a very tough, uphill battle.

What advice would you give someone who wants to be a jingle writer?

Probably no different from any other business: Do everything you can as well as you can. You can always at least lay your head down at night knowing you didn't have to compromise. You will know that you did your best even if you lose out to another company. Also, get your business chops together.

The big thing I think is listening. I am amazed at people writing stuff and they don't seem to hear the other things around them. I don't mean to plagiarize or steal; but boy, if you don't know what is current and contemporary you are not going to succeed. Keep listening. I've spent hundreds and hundreds of hours recording other people's jingles. I hire friends who record TV commercials in their regional markets to bring them back here and dissect them. It is interesting to listen to national jingles and ask, "Why does that sound different?", constantly comparing our productions to things that are out there.

What about apprenticeship or schools that teach this?

I am not aware of any schools that really teach this. There are a couple of books that are advertised in the music magazines and a few tapes available on the subject. It's really not that much different from songwriting in that a jingle is a 30-second song. You're writing the hook, writing chords, and maybe a verse.

Can a hopeful jingle writer gain recognition by submitting a tape to an advertising agency?

Absolutely. And submitting it again and again and again. Persistence is important. I am still opening doors that I first knocked on 10–12 years ago.

◊ *ARRANGER*

The arranger is a composer of sorts who writes parts to complement the songwriter's work. When a songwriter finishes a song, a rough version is recorded and commonly referred to as the "demo." It might simply consist of the songwriter singing along with a piano or a guitar or it might be a well-produced version with multi-instrumental accompaniment. The demo is given to the artist and producer who will be recording the master version for commercial purposes. The producer uses this version as a guide during pre-production work and may refer to it during the actual recording session. The songwriter's melody and chord changes remain unchanged, but the arrangements usually differ from the original.

There are a couple of ways a producer can communicate to the musicians about how song is to be performed. First, the producer can play the song for the musicians and have them "take down" the chord changes and form. Then, as a team led by the producer, they will work out the arrangement. Second, the producer can hire an arranger to notate the music for the session musicians. The arranger's job could be as simple as taking down the chord changes and having them copied for the musicians or as complex as writing out every note for every player on the recording session.

The most common practice is to combine both techniques. The arranger makes a sketch of the tune with the appropriate chord changes and pertinent musical passages and the studio musicians listen to the demo before they play it. This helps them get the "feel" of the song. The arranger is often not brought in until the basic tracks for a record are laid down and it is time to add strings, horns, or background vocals. The arranger writes out these parts to complement what is already on the tape.

My former employer, Kenny Rogers, occasionally had the opportunity to use supplemental musicians for a television show or special event. When we performed on *The Tonight Show* and used the fine musicians in the NBC Orchestra, one of my jobs was to arrange the "charts" for them. I would listen to a recording (usually a cassette tape in those days) of our group playing the song, then I would compose lines, melodies, harmonies, etc. for the orchestra to complement what we were already playing and what Kenny was singing. The most challenging arranging job I had was to arrange Kenny's entire live show for the Atlanta Symphony Orchestra when they joined us for a summer pops concert.

A successful arranger needs some schooling. It is very difficult to pick up a pencil and start writing for all the various instruments without a basic knowledge of the ranges, tonal characteristics and other idiosyncrasies of those instruments. Most music schools offer courses in orchestration or arranging that anyone serious about this career should take. However, a college education is not the last word; it merely gives you some basic tools to work with.

Practical experience is essential and one way to get it is by hanging out with and learning from an arranger who is doing some good work. When I was younger I had the good fortune to be taken under the wing of the late Bill Justis, a wonderfully gifted composer and arranger from Nashville, who taught me a lot just by allowing me to watch him work. Even though I have a degree in music, I still consider the time that I spent with him my most valuable learning experience in arranging. There also are several books on the subject. I especially recommend *Sights and Sounds* by Henry Mancini.

Arrangers are paid on the basis of output; therefore, it is necessary to develop speed in writing the music in order to become financially successful. This is a laborious process but can be developed with practice. When I arrange a series of tunes I usually find the last few go much faster than the first few because by the time I am towards the end of the project I am up to speed. The musician's union has different scales for recordings, television, live performance, etc., and the rate is based on four bars of music (referred to as a page of music). Some of the most successful arrangers earn incomes in the six-figure range.

Some arrangers do symphonic work, some orchestrate for film and TV, others transcribe arrangements for high school and college bands, orchestras, and jazz ensembles. Each requires the same basic skills and, depending on your musical tastes, each can be rewarding for the arranger.

Interview with Jeremy Lubbock
Arranger

Perhaps the most noted arranger in the business, Jeremy Lubbock has a client list that reads like the Who's Who *of popular music. His British wit and depth of knowledge made for an interesting and informative interview.*

Tell me what you do.

I do a number of things: I arrange, produce, and write songs.

This interview will be about arranging. Tell me about that.

There are two schools of thought about this. One is that you do it in a reasonably conventional way, which is you go to school and learn how to do it. The other is that you teach yourself how to do it. I think it is fair to say that if you've got reasonably good ears, it's possible to do that. The advantage of not going to school is that your style tends to be much more personal. You are not following anybody's rules. There are basically no rules in music except what your ear tells you. All this crap about not having parallel fifths is absolute nonsense – Who says? God never said you couldn't have parallel fifths.

I sort of knew in the back of my mind that even if I had the choice of going to school, I wouldn't have taken it. For what it is worth I would say that it is better to be individualized. Being in a business that can be so competitive, you have to sound like something special, otherwise you will just get eaten up in everybody else's work.

What do you have to know in order to do what you do?

First of all, I had certain advantages. I come from a very musical family. I am one of five children. My father was not a professional musician, but a very fine, talented musician. I mean really extraordinary. My three sisters and I were a string quartet. We used to play, but we used to play without music. At the age of 7 or 8, somebody would suggest a melody that we all knew and we would

32

make up harmonies. It was a completely natural thing for us to do. When I went to what is the equivalent of your high school, I played in the orchestra as a violinist. I played Brahms symphonies; we didn't mess around with Sousa and stuff like that.

So, having grown up in a musical house and having played in an orchestra, not only do I know what an oboe sounds like, but I know what it is supposed to be doing. It's not supposed to be doing the same thing that a flute's doing because it's a different instrument; it's a different animal. The French horn is not supposed to do the same as the bassoons. It's a question of knowing the cast of characters, and how to make them shine. What is it that makes them sound the best, how do you write for each instrument to make them sound the best, what is the basic character of the instrument? So, that you have to know. It's extraordinary how many people I come across in the business who don't really know what things sound like.

Did you learn to read music in high school?

I still can hardly read it, but I can write it. Set me down at the piano and I go, what?? But I learned to know it and to write it out.

Where did you learn how to transpose?

I don't.

You write them out in concert pitch?

Oh, absolutely. Except I have occasionally, on some really big scores for symphonies, burned my brains out and transposed everything. You see, what you don't know is that I started out life as an architect. So I have a very sharply defined visual sense. My eyes are as sharp as my ears. I need to be able to see a score. The French horns are written a fifth higher than they sound, but I want to be able to see where they are playing. I've got to see it. It drives me crazy when you read miniature scores and everything is in a different key. Yes I know how to do it, but I don't do it.

So if I were starting a record project, at what point would I call you?

That depends how good a producer you are. The single biggest mistake is made when a producer gives you a track to work with and there is no room on it for strings. They are so busy filling it up with guitar licks and synthesizer parts, and God knows what. About half the time, the only time I hear my arrangements is when I go away from the studio where I have just cut it with a rough mix cassette on which the strings are clear. Then three months later I go to the record store and I buy the record and they are gone. It's not just that they are quiet; they are gone. I think, why do you spend all that money if you don't want to hear it?

If you are good producer you call me in when you have a very basic track with vocals. Some people send me tracks without the vocals and I have a hard time explaining to them why it is that I need the vocals. So if they are sensible they call me when they have a basic track then after you have done the strings, then you put the guitar licks on it depending on how much space you have left on the tape. There's only room for a certain amount of frequencies. Of course, there are no limits to the amount of tracks you have, but after a while the frequencies all start fighting with each other.

Do you have a philosophy about what works and what doesn't as far as string arrangements are concerned?

The problem is, Edgar, you see, every single project that you are faced with is different, the singer is different, the song is different, the track is different, the key is different. So it is very, very hard to make generalizations. But, what you do learn is that the track dictates very much how you write your chart. Because there are certain string things that, in order to be heard, you need a good deal of space. If you do a lot of internal writing with strings you've got to have space to be heard; otherwise, they get eaten up. So if you have a very thick track, you do incredibly simple things that you know will be heard. The most obvious one is to have the entire string orchestra just play in octaves. That is always going to be heard, particularly if the track is very thick. If the track is transparent or there is room on the tape then you can do the more interesting stuff.

Tell me how you got a start and got established as the arranger that you are. What did you have to go through to get where you are?

A good deal of luck. I came to America without any work at all. Nothing, absolutely nothing. I didn't have a work permit; I didn't have any work. I only knew one person who was in the industry and that was Henry Lewy, who in those days was Joni Mitchell's producer and engineer. I met him through a friend and I did some demo work. Then I worked with Joni on that record she made with Charlie Mingus.

Then Henry was hired to produce the last record that Minnie Ripperton ever made. He took me to Minnie's house to meet her husband, Dick, who is a very good friend of mine. I played them some of the stuff I'd done in England. Then they hired me to do the entire record, everything, rhythm, brass and strings. It created quite a stir. Quite a few people heard it who liked it a lot, and thought it was unusual. That basically is what got it started. The word spreads out that there is someone new in town and they love that. So that was the catalyst that started it.

In the last few years there has been a lot of digital sampling and the synthesizer stuff. Has that affected your work as an arranger?

Yes, I would say so, particularly with the advent of sampling because people think they can do string charts just by playing them on a Synclavier. It doesn't sound the same, but they don't know that. I think the pendulum is going to swing back in the industry.

Is most of your arranging for record dates?

Yes.

Who are the artists you've worked with?

Well, there is almost nobody that I haven't worked with.

What would you tell somebody that wants to be a successful string arranger?

First of all, they have to realize what it takes to understand the strings. There is something special about arranging for strings. In order to know that, it is very important that you listen to some very significant music that has been written over the years in the classical field. There are certain composers that were just masterful at it. You have to know this music and understand it. Elgar was probably as good as there ever has been, and Vaughn Williams. There is some wonderful string music by Bartok; there is also wonderful string music by Mozart, Bach, and those people. As far as relevance to writing for records and the like, I don't think Mozart and Bach have that much to do with it, but Elgar and Ravell certainly do.

I think one of the advantages I have is my whole European background in string music. Most here just don't have it and it does sound different. I think it was that sound that originally attracted people to what I was doing. Though they didn't know that is what they were interested in.

So you would recommend someone listen to and get acquainted with the European style?

Yes, it is essential. There is no 19th-century American music; there is only 20th-century. There's Copeland and Charles Ives, and all those people, but there is no American equivalent to Elgar. There is another thing I have never been able to understand: The Americans are unbelievably disdainful of English music. It is stupid is what it is, because they miss a terribly important segment of music. It is certainly important to what I do. I think it's also important that

35

arrangements are positively created rather than just being there. It shouldn't be like wallpaper. One should actually create the atmosphere for that song. I think you have to treat it like a very serious piece of music. It can't be done in just one morning.

How long does it take you to do an average arrangement for a record?

Oh, I would say a couple of days. I like to let it cook. I don't like to rush it. I believe the people contracting you want you to take the time as well. You can hear a chart that's done in just a morning or one that has been written in two days. There's a big difference.

◊ COPYIST

When the arranger finishes his/her job, the score is handed to the music copyist who writes out the individual parts for the musicians. This is no small job and involves much more than copying notes from the score. The transcriptions must be accurate, legible, and easy for musicians to understand. The copyist must study musical form, notation, and the use of symbols in written music. There are several helpful books on the market: One is *The Art of Music Copying*. Like most jobs in the music business, the trade can be learned by apprenticeship. When I learned arranging from the late Bill Justis, his copyist, Jack Martin, taught me the basics of music copying.

In the past, most music for commercial recordings and live orchestra was written by hand with a pen and ink. Commercially produced arrangements were copied with a music typewriter. Now, a copyist can create commercial quality parts by using music copying software, such as Finale or Sibelius on a Mac or PC.

The music copyist is paid per page of music copied. As with arranging, the rate varies according to its use. Quality and output are the keys to being a financially successful copyist. Most copyists who live in a recording town such as Los Angeles, New York, or Nashville can make a decent living.

Interview with Eberhard Ramm
Music Copyist

Eberhard Ramm was trained as a French horn player and was principal horn in the Nashville Symphony from 1969 to 1978. In addition, he taught private lessons at the Blair School of Music at Vanderbilt University, where he also performed with the Blair Woodwind Quintet and the Nashville Contemporary Brass Quintet. Active as a player in the Nashville recording studios for 25 years, he branched out

*into music preparation, arranging and conducting. He has a 15 golf handicap –
and you can see some of his work at www.aardworks.com.*

Tell me about being a music copyist and what it takes to do that.

Well, it's totally changed from when I started, obviously. When I started it
was all by manuscript, which is a completely lost art now. In the last 20 years,
computers have taken over. So you have to have a certain amount of computer
knowledge, and that seems to be increasing into all types of other programs
outside of just music notation programs. But you don't have to be a total
computer geek – the operating systems are so stable and the software is good
enough where you'll get good results without having to know a whole hell of a
lot about computers.

But I must say that I think the manuscript experience – the experience of
visualizing it and then drawing it – was really helpful to me when I went over
to do it on the computer. There's a certain feel that it instills in you in terms of
how things should look – what looks good to the player. There are a lot of people
doing this on computers now that really spit out some pretty horrible-looking
stuff. So it's a matter of having a good eye for layout – that's a big part of it. And
then you apply all of your musical skills so you can help arrangers find and
fix mistakes and minimize your own mistakes, because if you understand the
context of the music it makes you do a much better job.

So some knowledge about theory, orchestration, and things like that are
really, really helpful to have, and probably essential to doing a good job in any
kind of big-time way.

And the other main thing is just patience. The copyists are always the last guys
to have their hands on things before the concert, or the session, or whatever, and
it tends to be last minute. So you have to be really efficient in order to be able to
handle that kind of stuff. But you still have to be really patient; otherwise, you
can make some really bad mistakes.

Now, you came to this business years ago through being an instrumentalist?

No, I wouldn't say that. I got started – I think you'll find this interesting
– I got started because of Irving Kane (laughter). (Note: Irving Kane was a
notorious Nashville trombone player. –Ed.) He got an arranging job from a guy
who was writing a musical about Jesus called *The Carpenter's Son*, and Irving
didn't know any copyists. He'd never been hired to do anything like that and
his own compositions, he'd just scratch them out himself. We were just sitting
around talking about it, and I said, "Heck, I'll do it," 'cause I'd done that sort of
thing for myself for little arrangements I'd written over the years. So I did the
job, and Buddy Skipper (Nashville arranger and music director. –Ed.) saw the

copywork I did on that, and he was looking for a copyist and so he hired me. I just kind of layered on to that. So it was a complete coincidence, really.

How long ago was that?
That was in 1973? 1974?

Prior to that time, you were in the music business as a what?
I was the first horn player in the (Nashville) Symphony at that time.

What were some of the specific things you needed to learn to be a copyist?
Well, I'd been exposed to enough symphonic music and chamber music and all that stuff – I'd been doing that since I was a kid. So I just had a pretty good idea about what needed to go on the page – places where people needed cues so they wouldn't get lost and the relative size and importance of various pieces of information. I had a good sense of that.

Well, you must have, because most people don't – they're not intuitive about things like that.
You have to help guide the musicians whenever possible. In session playing where you don't normally cue a lot of stuff, double bars and those kinds of things are really important to have in the right place. And you break up the multi-measure rests in the right place. If you're counting rests and you have four bars then five bars, and the trumpets come in real loud on the fifth bar, you take out a pencil and you scribble in "trumpet." Then you always know where you are. As a copyist, even if you don't give them the cue, you give them the road map so they can write it in and the player can feel his way comfortably though what's going on. And you make sure you don't put the multi-measure rest across phrases. You let the musicians use what I call their innate musicality. You have to use your observation of what's going on to help the players who don't have the benefit of having the whole score in front of them.

Did you pick up any of your skills by means of a mentor or by reading?
You know, I didn't. But there are some books out there – I know there used to be one – a book for manuscript purposes – years ago. It was a book where this guy had set down some hard and fast rules.

I believe I have that book. It's called **The Art of Music Copying,** *by Clinton Roemer. (Now out of print, but still available used from Amazon.com. –Ed.)*
Yeah, that's probably it. I never read that. Again, I just trusted the fact that I had seen so much printed music – I was a music geek growing up. I was around

music four or five hours a day. So I've seen a lot of printed music. All different kinds – I looked at scores, and I play piano, horn. So I got a really good idea of what needed to be on the page, and at the time, I had a really good hand, too. A lot of people really liked my manuscripts.

So a certain amount of artistic ability was part of the drill, right?

Yes. A meticulous hand was really important. George Tidwell (Nashville trumpeter and copyist. –Ed.) used to get these fancy little rulers that he could slide across the page. He'd make the stems and crescendos all real nice and even-looking. In those days we used to use onionskin. (A type of semi-transparent paper, also known as vellum. –Ed.) You'd make a cheater – you'd go through the three trumpet parts and whatever they had in unison, you'd put on the onionskin. Then you would print it up on regular paper and then fill in the rest of it. So back in that day, you had to have a really great spatial sense of where stuff was going to be on the page. And again, now the computer does help you do that.

Now, if you were just starting out, where would you go to learn about this?

I would just go back to published, printed material and be as observant as possible about where stuff goes. Looking at all the details, looking at a lot of different material.

There's one particular book out that I've read quite a bit about. Something like *Finale Productivity*, and I think it's available online. (*Finale Productivity* by Bill Duncan, book and CD-ROM. See http://www.npcimaging.com/books/BillDuncan.htm. –Ed.) It goes into a lot of detail about how to get the most out of Finale. (Finale is music manuscript software that is arguably the industry standard. –Ed.) Actually, if I were starting out now, I think I would use Sibelius. (Sibelius is also music manuscript software. –Ed.) I think most people are in agreement that it's easier to use. And like I say, try to study whatever you can get your hands on.

If you're in a town that does recording sessions, try to get a professional copyist to show you some stuff. I would also think there probably are classes in colleges and universities that have music departments. (Online research shows there are indeed classes. –Ed.)

Tell me what a typical project looks like when it comes in the door. Can you describe the process from start to finish?

Well, if it's an orchestral thing, then it comes in as a big, handwritten score, with all the shortcuts an arranger can possibly take. If it's a single arrangement, you just deal with one file. But if it's a series of arrangements, which it so often is, then the first step for me is to make a template for that project. And spend some time with it and hopefully catch every little nuance. Make sure you get all the instruments named right, and all their transpositions taken care of, and any other things that are going to be recurring in that project. The template needs to have that. Set up whatever your playback instruments will be for listening back. And then you save it as whatever the title is of the song.

And you just start from it – I lay out where all the double bars are and the tempo markings – that's the first pass. And then the second pass is putting in pitches, and then you have a pass where you edit those pitches with whatever information – dynamics, articulation – that kind of thing. Then I do a proofreading pass, which would include a playback – just listening for any glitches. Then, an actual, physical pass of visually checking everything. And then you have to create the parts and lay them out. And then you print the parts.

Actually, what I do is I print them to 8 ½ by 11 and I have a copier designated for the purpose of blowing them up to 9 ½ by 12 ½-inch paper. So I blow them up 89 percent so they fill up a music stand. It's more or less the size of standard manuscript paper. 8 ½ by 11 looks dinky on a music stand. There's no need to do that.

And scores can be all sorts of different sizes. A very good size for scores with larger instrumentation is 11 by 14. It fits on a music stand pretty well. The 11 by 17 gets real floppy. And also, I print it on heavier stock – 32-pound, laser print-quality paper. It sits on a music stand – it won't fall over. Then for theater projects that are going to run for an extended period of time, I have to use a heavier stock than that, like a hundred-pound text, which can take months and months of abuse.

Is here anything else you'd like to add?

I think one of the main things for people to know about this particular line of work is that a lot of times it functions under extreme time pressure. I just did a recent project for the Old Globe Theater in San Diego. They just opened a production of *Sammy*, which is about Sammy Davis Jr. All the vocals would be changed all the time. That went on for about a month – all the little vocal lead sheets. And then I got into the orchestrations, and that lasted another month. Leslie Bricusse, he wrote the show. There are 25 songs for a 13-piece pit orchestra. And I worked for two solid months, seven days a week. Most days I worked double-digit hours in order to bring home that project. That's the nature of the beast.

It also tends to be "feast or famine." This gig came on the heels of having absolutely nothing come across for January and February. Now, that was because of the economy, primarily. Somebody who is high-strung and can't deal with the time pressures and those kinds of issues definitely should not be in this line of work.

<u>ON RECORD</u>

*Music Publisher, Record Producer, Recording Engineer,
Artist & Repertoire (A&R), and Record Promoter*

It isn't an accident when a tune climbs to No. 1 on the charts. A whole team of people has worked very diligently on that tune since it was written. The record industry, viewed by some as a looming enigma, is actually quite understandable and accessible once it is broken down into the various parts that make up its whole. The different departments, perhaps manned by musicians who for whatever reason have gravitated toward the business side of music, all work together to find talent, match songs with the talent, record the songs, promote, market, and sell the finished product: a record.

Here is a look at some of the job opportunities in the recording industry.

MUSIC PUBLISHING

Music publishing is the business of getting a product – in this case a song – in front of the public and collecting the money that is generated as a result of public consumption. The music publisher works with the songwriter to develop songs, perhaps tailoring them to meet the needs of a particular artist or situation. The publisher then "pitches" songs to recording artists, which is arguably the most important function.

A songwriter can write songs until blue in the face, but those efforts are futile if there is no way to get these tunes recorded. Hopefully, the publisher has enough connections in the recording industry to get the writer's tunes in front of artists and producers.

Publishers also negotiate fees and collect money for the various ways a song may be used. For example, if a song is used in a motion picture, the publisher negotiates those fees with the movie producers. The publisher may also be responsible for advising the performance rights societies when the writer's tunes are used in a TV show.

There are three performance rights societies in the United States: ASCAP, BMI, and SESAC. They all serve the same function: to monitor airplay and other public performances of music, collect fees from users, and distribute the money to the writers and music publishers. (See Resources for information on performance rights societies.)

There is considerable money in music publishing if you have the wherewithal to get your songs recorded and played on radio or TV. A publisher can expect to make several thousand dollars from a tune that gets Top 40 airplay, or as much as several million from a tune like "The Gambler," which has not only been played on the radio, but was the title song for five TV movies and the theme music for many other events. Publishers are also always happy to have their tunes used in national advertising campaigns, which can generate up to six-figure fees.

Music publishers should have sound business knowledge and a keen ear for commercial music. Business knowledge can be obtained by getting a degree with an emphasis in music business. A good ear for commercial music, however, comes from years of experience in the business.

You can get a business degree in music from several colleges, such as Belmont College in Nashville, Tennessee. You can get experience in the publishing business by signing on with a publisher to do menial tasks: making CD copies, typing lyric sheets, etc., starting at the bottom and working your way to the top. You must be able to work well with people because that is what the publishing business is all about – interacting with writers, recording artists, and producers. It is essential to establish contacts in the industry, just as in any other business, and this takes time.

The publishing business can be very expensive. There are recording costs, writer's salaries (draw against royalties), and other general expenses. However, profits can be enormous if a publisher manages to have a few hits or places his music in a long-running television series.

Want to start your own publishing company? It is not that hard to do, but getting to the point where the royalties are pouring in is a whole different story. Learn as much as you can about the business first by working in a publishing house. As your understanding of the business grows, find a writer that you believe in that is new in town and hasn't been signed. Get that person (who could be *you* if you are a writer and want to self-publish) to agree to sign over the publishing rights to his songs to you in exchange for your shopping or "pitching" the tunes to all the artists and producers you can get to. Select a name for your company and clear it with ASCAP, BMI, or SESAC. Start knocking on doors, dropping off CDs, sending out MP3s, and networking with other publishers, writers, producers, artists, and managers. This is shoestring-budget publishing, by the way. If you are fortunate to get a cut that brings in some decent royalties, maybe then your business could afford to put your writer(s) on a draw, and maybe hire some administrative people. It is much easier to get your songs to the right people if they know you're professional and in it for the long haul.

Interview with Ree Guyer
Wrensong Publishing

What is your background?

I'm from St. Paul, Minnesota, and went to St. Mary's College in Winona, Minnesota, where I studied studio arts and psychology for a double major. My main focus was as a potter. I had been a potter from age 15 until I graduated from school and that is what I did every summer. My father was a writer and a musician and had a lot of success being a toy and game inventor. I had sung on several things and written a lot with him throughout my childhood. So hanging out with him in all the studios in that area, I knew many musicians and writers. He had a catalog of about 10 songs. There were two other writers who had about 10 songs each so we started with 30 songs. It was out of a need that my father and these writers had to get their songs out. They were doing wonderful demos out of a really fine studio in Minneapolis, Sound 80, where Michael Johnson, Melissa Manchester, and Jim Croce also worked out of.

My father hired a woman to plug his songs. After three months she said, "Forget it, I can't get into any of these doors and I don't want to do this." I said to my father, "Hey, I know all these musicians, all these writers, let me try to do something with these songs." He agreed and so I started this venture (at this point on a part-time basis) by getting a list from Michael Johnson of about 12 or 15 publishers. These were publishers that he had worked successfully with over the years in Nashville. He gave me the list and said to go for it. I got to know these publishers and started sending them songs.

The songs I had were great songs. They weren't just OK songs. I would say that three out of the 10 (per writer) were just great songs. I was pitching those songs and the doors were really opening for me; but I was pitching them to publishers because I wasn't set up to be a publisher. I was only an agent for these writers.

After about a year and half of that (still part-time), during which time I made two trips to Nashville, I realized that I should try to get in to see the producers and A&R people at the labels myself. To find more great songs and great writers that we knew were in the Twin Cities area, I organized a seminar that took about six months to put together. I invited all the people that I had met in

Nashville. Fortunately writers Kye Fleming and Dennis Morgan had become good friends and they were really hot then. They agreed to come up and also Joe Moscheo from BMI, John Sturdivant from ASCAP, and a couple of other publishers/producers. They all agreed to come and up and do the seminar. I also got entertainment lawyers, booking agents, and managers from the area to do the seminar. That was in 1983. That's where I met John Vezner and we started working together at that point. I met another fellow, John Kurhajetz, who wrote "Gonna Take a Lot of River" done by the Oak Ridge Boys.

After we did the seminar, in 1984 we got our first cut, an Oak Ridge Boys record, "Little Things," that went No. 1 for us. That was one of the three "great" songs that I mentioned before that I had been pitching for a year and a half.

So at that point we decided we needed to move here (Nashville) and we needed to start a publishing company. We moved at the end of 1984 and established our company in 1985, and that is when we signed our first writers: John Kurhajetz and John Vezner.

I really believe that you have to physically be here to make things happen. Once we moved here it just exploded. We had three singles our first year. That was the only way we made money as a publisher back then, that is to have our songs released as singles. Now you can make money just having cuts because there are so many records being sold. (Even if a song is not released as a single you still receive license royalties for each unit sold.)

What does it take to be a good publisher?

You have to have great songs. For example, I just knew the song "Little Things" was a great song because it just made my insides tingle. It made me feel good. It was separated in a way from the other songs because it was so good. It caused an emotional response for everyone that heard it.

Even with a good song, as a publisher, you still have to be very persistent. You must never forget how you felt when you first heard that song because you have to play it so many times for so many people. You must remember that this is the first time they have heard the song. Hopefully they will feel how you felt and get excited about the song. You just have to be very, very persistent. I pitched that song hundreds of times before it got cut. Timing has a lot to do with it too, but you can ensure good timing if you are really persistent and keep pitching and pitching your song.

"Gonna Take A Lot of River" was an unusual song but I felt the same way about it as I did about "Little Things." It made people happy and made people smile. There was an emotional reaction when you played it for people. I knew the minute I heard it it was going to be a single and it was going to be a big

45

record. I kept playing it for people and they would say, "No, Ree, this is too different," "No, I don't know who would cut this," "No, this is weird."

I got many "No's" but one person at MCA was looking for songs, and I never forgot the first time that I played the song for him he loved it. So I decided to keep pitching it to him until he found an act at MCA that would cut it. Over the course of a year I pitched it to him six times on six different occasions.

Every time I pitched other songs to him I also pitched "Gonna Take a Lot Of River." The sixth time the Oak Ridge Boys were across the street in the studio looking for up-tempo songs. He took it right over there and they cut it within a couple of weeks. It was a No. 1 record for them and somewhat brought their career back.

Another example was "Train Wreck of Emotions," Lorrie Morgan's first single and big record. I felt the same thing about that song. It was up-tempo, a little bit different and had something special about it. When a writer writes a song like that, I'm on sort of rampage about it for about a month. I'll keep pitching it and pitching it and pitching it to everybody in the business, and then I'll do it again and make sure everybody hears it again. I started doing my rounds with the song and took it to Mary Martin at RCA. She loved it and said she would give it to Barry Beckett who was producing several acts for them. I ended up going to play songs for Barry a couple of days later, and when I walked in his secretary said he had passed on the song, "Train Wreck of Emotions." I said, "He can't pass on this song; it's a great song," so I took it back into the meeting with me and Barry listened to it again. I said to him "It's a hit even though you may not have an artist for it, but I know it's a hit." So he played it again and he said, "Ree, you're right. It's a hit but I already have a song with a train in it on hold for Lorrie." I said, "Well, just play it for her." He did and she loved it as much as this other train song so the two train songs ended up going to Joe Galante and he ended up picking up our song. It was her first single and her album went gold.

It really is just persistence. There are so few songs in your catalog that you know are great, that really stand out. There are many good songs but the great ones I am really persistent with.

What services do you perform for a writer besides song plugging?

I think the most important thing we do for writers is act as a PR agent for our writers. I have six writers and some writer/artists, but all told I probably have 10 writers. Every day I am promoting these writers and talking about them to record labels, to producers, to managers, to artists. I talk to others about how they write, their songs, about their track records.

We also give a service in that we support a writer, not a heavy amount of money but we support them so they can just write. We give them draws so they can focus on writing and we give them demo budgets so they can demo any song that we feel is fit to be demoed.

Can you comment on becoming a writer?

I really think that to make it as a professional writer it is very important to find a person that believes in the way you write. Initially that might just be a publisher that knows you have potential. When I first came to town I had more time to spend with writers that I felt had potential and would be great writers someday. I nurtured several of those writers. I would critique their songs and eventually I ended up signing those writers.

Sandy Ramos was one of those writers. I would evaluate her songs and give advice like, "It's good but you can do better," or "You're not quite right on the choruses yet." I watched her and nourished her for a couple of years and finally ended up signing her. She has since become one of my biggest writers.

As a writer, search out a person who believes in what you are doing. Talk to BMI or ASCAP because they know the publishers who are looking for new writers and who are looking to nurture new writers.

What would you tell someone coming out of high school or college about how they can start in the publishing business?

If you want to be a publisher I think there are a couple of ways to learn this part of the business. I was fortunate because I had the backing and you can't go into what I have done without the proper financial backing. You will fall on your face.

You need it to build a foundation, because I believe this business is built on relationships. You have to have enough time to nurture relationships so people respect who you are, what you do, and what kind of songs and talent you can find. The only way to build that is over time.

So if you're going the publishing route, find a writer that you really believe in, that you know has potential, and whose songs are better than some of the songs on the radio. Really work with that one writer.

Anybody can start nurturing relationships with record labels and producers because they are always looking for great songs. That is what everybody is looking for, great songs. It has nothing to do with the politics. A great song is a great song and it is going to find its way to the top. I believe that with all my heart.

Your company recently had a big record with Heart called "Stranded." How did this happen?

I had a meeting with Larry Hanby at CBS and played him the song. He was really emotionally moved by it and he said, "This is great. Rich Zito should hear this for Heart." Larry gave Richie a copy of it but we didn't hear anything for six to eight months. I was getting really frustrated, so I got hold of Richie's assistant and sent another copy to him overnight delivery. I didn't know if he had heard the song or if he even knew about it. He called me back the next day and said, "I have it and we're going to do a demo on it. I got it from Larry Hanby." Then it was a waiting game, which was really hard. We waited almost a year. There were 18 songs that they demoed and they put 13 on the album.

The same waiting thing happened with the single. They told us it would be one of the singles. They put the first single out, which didn't do much. Then they released the second single and it died a horrible and quick death. They quickly released our song to hopefully revive the album and it did! The song went to No. 10 on the CHR chart, No. 7 on AC and somewhere in the teens on the AOR charts.

◯ *RECORD PRODUCER*

I think of the producer as the "caretaker" of a record project. This person is involved from start to finish and is responsible for the outcome. When an artist makes a record, the producer selects and rents the studio, hires the engineer, the musicians that will be playing on the session, and the arranger (some producers do their own arranging). The producer is accountable for the way a record sounds and for helping the artist perform as well as possible. Sometimes a producer can get a vocalist to sing *better* than he or she thought possible! The record producer often selects the songs an artist will record. In some cases, song selection is collaboration between the artist and producer and, in other cases, it is strictly up to the artist.

However, the producer, the artist and the record company representative almost always agree on the songs to be recorded. A producer must know what constitutes a good commercial recording and which musicians are best suited for that particular type of music.

You can become a record producer by going to school to learn production techniques or by just hanging out in studios and watching other producers. An excellent starting place is to become an assistant to a producer. Becoming a recording engineer is a logical step towards becoming a producer, as is starting out as a studio musician. You must get as close to the recording business and/

or the people who are making records as you can. This could mean working as a receptionist at a studio or being a "runner" for a record company.

Producers are usually paid on a royalty basis, typically receiving three to four percent of the gross selling price of the album produced. They also may be paid an advance against royalties when the album is recorded. A successful producer who has records on the charts can make a six-figure income.

Interview with Barry Beckett
Producer

Starting out as a piano player in Birmingham, Alabama, Barry Beckett moved up through the ranks to become one of the most in-demand producers in the country. His work is evident on some of the most significant albums in rock and roll, country, and rhythm and blues. As we talked from his office on Music Row in Nashville, it became apparent to me that this man was responsible for writing some of the history of commercial music. This interview was conducted in the mid-1990s. In 2009, Barry passed away. He left an indelible mark on the music of the late 20th century, and his influences will be felt for many years to come.

How did you get started in the business?

I grew up in Birmingham and spent as much time as possible in studios and getting to know musicians. In high school and college, I played in bands. I got a degree in music theory (commercial music wasn't even taught then, unfortunately). After college our band did some recording for a small Muscle Shoals studio where they were just beginning to cut some hits. I was able to play on a record that went No. 1 called "I'm Your Puppet." That was the first hit I ever played on. I left the band and worked for a record producer for a while and eventually got hired back to the Muscle Shoals studio as a keyboard player. This was what I had hoped for – that is, making a living working in the studio full time.

Playing with a band is much different from playing individually. Once it clicked for us (the studio band) we starting cutting hits. We were a self-contained band. Very seldom would other musicians work with us. That was very unusual and lucky for us. Occasionally even in Nashville now, I am tempted to use the same bands on everything I record.

What hits did you cut at the Muscle Shoals studio?

Before I moved there, they had already recorded "Land of a Thousand Dances," "Mustang Sally," all the Wilson Pickett stuff and the very first Aretha Franklin stuff. Our band decided to go into the business with our own studio.

It took a year to cut a hit and that was "Take a Letter Maria." After this, the successes came in short spurts.

Paul Simon liked a song that we had recorded by the Staples, "I'll Take You There," which was based on reggae. So he booked four days to come in and record one of his songs. We cut the song in 30 minutes. He played a few songs on the piano for us and asked us which other ones we wanted to work on. We said, "OK, let's do 'Kodachrome,' 'One Man Sailing,' and a couple more." During those four days we cut half the album. The rest he completed in Los Angeles or New York.

Through working with Peter of Peter, Paul, and Mary, I met Mary McGregor, who at the time was a background singer. Peter and another writer gave us a song for her, "Torn Between Two Lovers," which we recorded. This was the first No. 1 record I'd ever cut. This record went No. 1 on the pop charts and then No. 1 on the country charts. I realized from this that I could cut a hit in country music as well as pop.

Jerry Wexler brought a group to me called Sanford & Townsend and we cut "Smoke From a Distant Fire" in Muscle Shoals. I also got to work with Jerry on Bob Dylan's "Slow Train Coming" and "Saved." I also got to work with Dire Straits. Even though we didn't get a hit off of that album, it was a good album, and Mark Knopfler was great fun to work with.

How did you get to Nashville?

I had taken a year off, which gave me a chance to really think about where I was and what I really wanted to do. I wasn't interested in New York and I didn't want to go to Los Angeles because I didn't read music.

One day I heard Rodney Crowell on country radio with a very contemporary-sounding record, and I said, "Yeah, that's what I want to do." I also heard John Anderson's song, "Swinging," which is Southern rock, and that is what Muscle Shoals is about. So I got an apartment in Nashville and commuted from Muscle Shoals.

It took about a year, and as a result of some contacts I had made working with Delbert McClinton, I got to work with Jim Ed Norman on a Shelley West project. We got a Top 20 record, which helped prove to the country industry and myself that I could cut country records.

I also got to work with Karen Brooks through Jim Ed, which was a rather contemporary country project. After this, Jim Ed offered me the position as director of A&R, which I took. I will always be indebted to him because he gave me a chance in this town.

50

What about your philosophy on production?

I use great musicians that have fun and think of ideas on their own. To get really inspired playing, you have to go with their ideas as much as possible, and if it is going to work, it will work.

Stay honest and ethical. Stay away from politics. Go with the song and stick to an artist. That has worked for me so far.

What would you tell someone that would like to be a producer?

First, the strongest asset of a producer is a knowledge of songs. Second is the knowledge or ability to put a team together to get the record cut. You need to learn songs; I advise for someone to work in publishing. There, you will learn to work with writers and you will learn about doing demos. Doing the demos will acquaint you with the young musicians who will eventually become the great musicians. You'll learn by experimenting on putting things together, by arranging, and by doing some engineering. Even if you have to start by making tape copies, eventually you will make songplugger.

Another way to get started is to work at a record company. Gregg Brown, who is producing Travis Tritt, started out in the mailroom. As long as you do a good job, they know they can depend on you. If they know they can depend on you, then they are going to start paying you money for that dependability.

Interview with Danny Kee
Production Assistant/Warner Bros. Records

At the time of this interview, Danny was a recent college graduate, and well on his way to a successful career in the music business. He was the assistant to Jim Ed Norman, who at the time was president of Warner Bros./Nashville and one of the most respected and well-known producers in the business.

How did you get here?

I came here from Chicago. I went to college at Illinois State University and earned a bachelor's degree in business. I came to Nashville because I had heard about MTSU. (Middle Tennessee State University) Both of my parents were pro-education. Even though they didn't know anything about the recording business, they felt that it was important to get a proper education. They felt also that a university could help get me into an internship in the business world. That is what I did. I came to MTSU and took a couple of semesters of classes there – just enough to build my knowledge of the recording industry.

Fortunately I wasn't trying to earn a second bachelor's degree, so I had the opportunity to go to college and take only the classes I wanted to take. I took recording engineering with a little electronics thrown in. I am not an engineer, but I do have a good understanding of how the equipment works. I know how the line path from microphone to tape works.

Along with that kind of education I also studied the legal aspects of the business. I took a couple of classes in contract law and copyright. I took a couple of publishing classes to understand how it relates to the writers, their relationships with the labels, getting songs recorded, and that sort of thing. I took music and some theory to brush up on that, because I don't think you can ever get enough of that.

I am not a professional musician and my abilities in music are limited. I've always played instruments, played in bands in high school, but I've never done it professionally. I just got in the business end of things.

How did you get your basic interest in the music business?

I was in a band that I would call sub-professional, not even semi-professional. I was a drummer in a band for a long time through high school, but I gave it up when I went to college, dismissing music and art as something at which you couldn't earn a living. My parents persuaded me to go into business, which they thought was more stable. They were looking out for my best interests since they did come from poor backgrounds and wanted more for me, essentially.

So in the middle of getting my business degree in college, I started working with a band doing sound and booking dates and kind of acting as a manager for them. That is how I got involved in the business. The more I hung out with people that did that sort of thing, the more I found that there were other things in the recording industry to do besides being a player. There are producers, people who do promotion, marketing, publicity, publishing, people who run recording studios, and engineers. There are tons of things that go on besides the people who actually sing and play.

What is your ultimate goal?

My initial goal was to be a record producer. After going through college and interning with Warner Bros., the more interest I had in being a producer but also in being in the A&R department. There you work with artists collecting songs, signing artists, putting artists together with producers to create the product, and working with them creatively. I have a high degree of interest in that because I don't believe I'd want to be an independent producer spending all my time in the studio. A position at the label in addition to producing records would be ideal for me.

Tell me about your internship at Warner Bros. How did that come about?

The internship program was through college, and the whole point of it is to try to get students into positions in the recording industry making a living. Unfortunately, there are many more students at college studying the recording industry than there are positions to accommodate those people. I knew in school that I was up against a rigorous and competitive field.

When I finished with the courses I wanted to take, I applied for an internship. Specifically I went to Warner Bros. because of my interest in the company and their artists. There was a line out the door of people hoping to get this position where they would work without a salary yet get college credit and learn the business first hand. A friend of mine who finished school a little earlier than I had been interning at Warner Bros. and had just gotten a job working on the pop promotion staff there. He recommended me for the position and I was accepted by Warner Bros.

What did your internship involve?

When I first started I was working in the A&R department and they had me doing very menial things. I accepted this, knowing that's the way any industry works. You have to earn trust. When I first started, I was given boxes of tapes that we had listened to in our A&R department. I called the people whose names were on the tapes to tell them that their songs had been rejected. Essentially these were called "pass calls." I spent day in and day out on the telephone giving out the bad news. Most of the people were thankful that we even called back to say we had passed.

Even though it seemed like a thankless, tedious job, it really had a hidden benefit in that I learned all the names of all the publishers, writers. I got to know them as a result. This has paid off since I started working at Warner Bros. with Jim Ed. If we needed a song, or wanted to hold a song, or if we needed a meeting, it was extremely helpful to know these people. Anyway, I licked envelopes, sorted mail, answered phones, and did a lot of busy work. I think the real key is being willing to do any job. The company takes note of that. If you did a good job, then they would start to give you other jobs with more responsibility.

I got to where I would listen to songs and decide if the material was quality material. I spent six to eight months doing that with no end in sight. Warner Bros. had made no promises, but I re-enrolled for another semester because I felt like something would have to open up even if it was in the mail room. I felt once I was in and getting paid, then I could work my way up.

One day when Jim Ed's secretary wasn't there to block the door, I poked my head in and asked if I could talk to him, and he invited me in. Even though I had already seen him at this point several times, I didn't know him very well.

I explained to him that I had been an intern there and that I really wanted to get into the business. I told him that I was ambitious and gung ho and I that I was willing to do anything even on a part-time basis. He reacted with a kind of standard answer: "I'm sorry but there isn't anything open." He kind of gave me a grim outlook on the situation, but I still wasn't prepared to quit at that. So I said, "OK, I understand, but if anything does open up in the future, please understand that I really want to be here and this is what I'd really like to do."

It wasn't even a whole week later that he called me at home one day and asked me to come to work for him directly as his assistant. He had been toying around with that as he needed to have somebody to help him with all the demands that were placed on him. It was an extremely lucky thing, but I believe it was because I had taken several initiatives, not only to get an internship, but to bust my butt while I worked at the internship, staying later and coming in early. I had been aggressive, not abrasive, and was vocal about what I wanted to do. I had many friends who wondered how on earth I got hired by a label while most of my college buddies were making tape copies for some publisher at $3 an hour. Here I was with a salary, a dental plan, and everything. I felt very fortunate and lucky, but you have to make your own luck and keep plugging away at it. I was ready to intern indefinitely if I had to. I had a job waiting tables at night that paid the rent. I felt like sooner or later they were going to have to hire another person, and I just knew that person would be me.

Have you done any producing since you have been at Warner Bros.?

Yes, I have had many opportunities. After following Jim Ed around now for about three years, booking musicians, booking studios, and handling all the paperwork and handwork and footwork it takes to produce a record, I have watched what he does and learned as much as I can. I talked with Jim Ed about what my goals were, and after a couple of years I got to work with a couple of artists that Warner Bros. was contemplating signing. We had a developmental deal; they would go in and do some demos, and based on those, they would be signed or not.

So I have done a little bit of that, and I have also gone out and tried to find some artists and get some money together to do some demos. I have only done that on a demo level, so I am still learning. I also had the opportunity to co-produce a Christmas record that children sang on with Jim Ed. It was an excellent opportunity for me to get my feet wet. His time is getting thinner and thinner; there are some things that he doesn't have the time to swallow so I ended up doing many of the day-to-day work with his guidance. I am in an excellent position working with Jim Ed because he believes in giving young people a chance.

◊ *RECORDING ENGINEER*

A recording engineer must be familiar with all the methods of recording music. There are schools that teach the techniques, but a lot of engineering is learned on an apprenticeship basis. Starting out, one might apply for a cleaning position just to get in the door. Sweeping floors might lead to what is called a "second" engineer position. The second is the person who helps the engineer by putting tape reels on the machine, cleaning the machine heads, setting up mics, and providing coffee for the clients. If the studio has digital recording equipment, the second might set up the templates for a recording session on the computer before the clients come in. The second does all of the legwork while the engineer does the knob turning. You will eventually work your way behind the board to do some engineering jobs.

If you'd rather not begin by sweeping floors, it's advisable to attend one of the recording schools. Most studios will not consider you for an apprenticeship unless you already know the basics.

It is important for recording engineers to have musical ability because they are often asked to determine whether a piece of music sounds right or whether a singer is in tune or not. When I produce records I always use someone familiar with music because I rely on the engineer to help me. No producer can catch every little thing all the time; it really helps to have a second set of good ears listening for mistakes or glitches in the recording. My engineer has often stopped the recording session and said, "Didn't you hear that little click in the track? I have to do it over again." It might have been caused by someone shuffling his or her feet or bumping the music stand. The engineer heard it but I missed it.

Changes are taking place in the recording business at a breathtaking pace. Digital recording technology has opened up a whole new world of recording techniques and gadgets that the engineer must become familiar with. New products come on the market every six months and the engineer must keep abreast of these changes to be competitive. It involves a process of continuing education. Trade publications and seminars help the engineer keep current. If you are considering a career as an engineer, it would be wise to get a copy of *Mix* magazine. It can be found in the waiting rooms of almost any major studio. If you are really dedicated, you'll be hanging out at the studios anyway, so pick up a copy and start reading.

Although some recording engineers make tremendous amounts of money, the typical engineer earns a middle-class income. Salaries range from $10,000 to $15,000 a year for an assistant just starting out and people who have advanced to full engineer status typically earn $30,000 to $40,000.

Interview with Linell
Assistant Engineer at a Nashville Recording Studio

From a background in music education, Linell has paid her dues, laid the groundwork, and gained an entry-level position in the recording industry. From here the only place to go is up!

How did you get interested in this business?

I have a music background and I used to teach in public school. I was at a point that I needed to progress and the progressions I saw in education weren't appealing to me, so I floundered for about eight months trying to figure out what it was I wanted to do. Then I saw an ad in a record store magazine for a school for recording engineers (The Recording Workshop) and I just knew that was what I wanted to do. I took all my retirement out of savings and spent it on this program. I loved it, but I wish it had been longer. I didn't want to go through another four-year program because I was too old for that. Seven weeks were not quite long enough, but I came to Nashville and got into the Castle Recording Studio as an intern.

How did you arrange that job?

After I got out of the workshop, I came to Nashville because I was somewhat familiar with it already, where I wasn't familiar with L.A. or New York. I knew I could get a job here. I worked at the Opryland Hotel in room service for a year just to pay the rent. With that job, I was off in the afternoon by 2 o'clock, so every day I would call someone in the engineering business and make an appointment. I didn't call as if I was looking for a job, I just said, "I'm new in town and I just got out of engineering school and I'm just trying to get to know people in the business and get advice. Could I spend 10 minutes with you giving me advice about how to get into this business?" Almost everybody would spend 10 minutes with me.

I got an annual *Mix* directory. (*Mix* magazine is a publication for audio/video recording engineers.) If the situation was comfortable with the person who gave me the appointment, I'd ask if I could sit in on a session sometime. If this was possible, then I'd come back and watch and learn and just try to get known around the community.

Through a referral, I met Dave S. at a studio. I let him know where I was coming from and he said that he couldn't pay me but I could help him out with live gigs around town that he did. Then I got an appointment with people at Castle. They were in fact looking for a new intern and at the same time putting in a new console and reconstructing the whole control room. The internship did not pay so I kept my day job and go straight from work to the Castle and spend another seven to eight hours over there. I did that for about eight months.

This job helped me get my foot in the door and 1) meet clients, producers, etc., and 2) read the manuals. When the sessions were a little slower, some of the engineers would take me under their wing (Castle is mostly a mixing studio) and let me come in and hang out, ask questions, check out the patch bay for the routing, and other things. So I learned a lot.

How did you get your current job?

Through Dave S., whom I had hooked up with a year before, so you never know. The idea for someone getting into this field is just to hook up with as many people as you can because you never know who and when it is going to be. I had worked with Dave on three sessions, live stuff, so he knew how I worked. People say over and over again, it is not so much your technical ability as it is your attitude and how much you really want to be here. He had gotten in with the people here and one of their backup engineers was leaving to go to law school, so Dave recommended that they call me. I have now been here about a year.

What do you do here?

When I am not doing session work, then I do tape vault inventory. For example, I am in the process of putting all information about the tapes on computer.

What do you do when you are assisting on a session?

I make sure all the machines are aligned, get the tapes set up with tones, get the room set up with reverbs, delays, and other equipment. It depends on the engineer. Some like you to have the whole thing set up, the cue mix, microphones, etc. Others want to tell you what mics, etc. to use. If he gives me a list of what he wants, then I just do the whole thing. Before he gets in the door, all the mics and headphones have been tested, there is a mix coming through, and tones are on the tape. Then they come in and get the sounds up.

Have you had any opportunity to do a session as the first engineer?

The chief engineer has encouraged me to bring in songwriter friends and be their engineer on demo projects. I have done three demo projects and those really helped me learn. My ambitions are to be the first engineer. With my musical ear, I have been encouraged to go for the producer's chair, but right now I am focused on being the first engineer.

Do you have to know how to fix the equipment?

I take care of headphones, cue boxes, and cables, some soldering. The other engineers fix a lot, but sometimes outside help has to be called.

Have you had any difficulties?

The hardest thing for me was learning the language. Kids I went to school with had been in bands and knew about guitars and amps, but I knew nothing. It was a whole new world to me and it was a whole different jargon, but I really love it!

◊ *A&R*

The A&R (artist and repertoire) job is a fairly critical position within the record company, as the A&R people function as the eyes and ears of the business. They are depended upon to bring new, exciting, and appealing talent to the company and to work closely with that talent to develop their music. This can mean working with the music publishers to help a particular act find new songs to record or perhaps assisting with the actual production process. The job sometimes involves traveling to other cities to hear new acts. One has to have an excellent ear for commercial music and a good feel for what the audience might like to hear (which translates into what the audience will buy). The quest for new talent also involves wading through piles of demo tapes, most of them pretty average sounding.

A&R people come from various backgrounds. Some start at the bottom and work their way up the ranks of the record company. Others graduate to A&R from production or management backgrounds. A performance background is a big help because creative types can be a particular breed and it sometimes takes one to know (and work with) one. To advance to an executive position in a record company, it is just about mandatory that one has had experience in A&R.

Interview with Dez Dickerson
V.P. of A&R, StarSong Records

Dez has had a very interesting career in music. For several years, he toured as lead guitarist for Prince. He has recently released a book about that experience, titled My Time With Prince, *and a solo album, and is currently president of Absolute Records. This interview was conducted during Dez's tenure at StarSong Records, a Christian label in Nashville.*

Tell me about your background.

I started out playing in little rock bands that I put together in high school when I was about 14 years old. I always had a desire and an ambition to play music as far back as I can remember. I used to watch Ozzie & Harriet and when Ricky would play, I thought that was cool and I wanted to do that. Through the Beatles and others, I really thought I wanted to be a musician, so I got serious about it. From ninth grade throughout high school my mother would write notes for me to be excused from school early on Friday so I could drive with my buddies out of town to play in some little town in North or South Dakota. (I am from St. Paul.) I pursued that course all throughout high school.

After I got out of school I had a full scholarship to go to computer school. I was trained as a computer technician and I graduated, but went full time into music. I pretty much made the decision at that point that music was what I was going to do for the rest of my life. That was about 1974.

About four years later, I had a chance to audition for a young man who at the time had done one record on Warner Bros. Records. He wasn't real well-known but was extremely talented, a guy named Prince. I auditioned for the gig and he asked me to learn some songs from his record. He called me up about a week later and asked me to come over to his house and jam with him and the bass player. That went on for probably about two months. He would call at least once or twice a week and I would go over to his house and we'd play some more. He never said that he was seriously considering me for the gig or anything. He'd just keep asking me to learn some more tunes and then come jam.

About two to two and a half months after I first auditioned, Prince's manager gave me a paycheck. That was the first I knew that I had the job. That set the tone for the next five years of my life. Pretty much from the first note that he played on stage as a Warner Bros. recording artist, I was with him at every gig he did. We did *American Bandstand, Midnight Special,* and all the shows that were around then. In 1981 we opened for the Rolling Stones. Before that we toured with Rick James and Tina Marie. In 1979 we did a video, before MTV. We pretty much went from the tour with Rick James and some occasional dates with Kool & the Gang and others to headlining. After the Stones thing we never opened for anyone again.

I continued with Prince through April 1983, did the 1999 album and tour, then I left for my own group which I had formed about a year and a half earlier. We did showcases in between Prince dates. We opened for Billy Idol in 1984, came off the road in September, and I did some studio things. I played on Aretha Franklin's "Freeway of Love" in 1985 or so.

I really kind of retreated from the business the next several years and started becoming involved in contemporary Christian music or gospel music, whatever you want to call it. I worked with an Atlantic artist named Judson Spence in 1987 who just recently finished his second album.

I began writing and producing for some Christian artists and that kind of segued into having relationships with a number of people in the Christian music industry which led to this position here at StarSong where I've been since April 1990.

Did you have any formal music training?

A little bit. I've always been more an ear and eye kind of guy. When I was young, theory and learning to read frustrated me. I just wanted to make music right away.

What are your responsibilities as an A&R person at StarSong?

There are several different strata of A&R people. There are A&R reps, A&R managers, A&R directors, etc. What I do here is kind of a combination of an A&R overseer and an A&R person. My title is V.P. of A&R and what I do is basically oversee the A&R department and help facilitate all that goes on that's product-related here at StarSong. I help choose producers, help oversee budgets and schedules.

I am directly involved in a finite number of projects each year where I am executive producer. I work with the artist, producer, outside writers, arrangers, engineers, and whoever else may be involved. I work with the logistics in terms of travel, scheduling, cash flow with the producer or artist or whoever is involved. I pretty much act as liaison, since the artist and the artist's interest are usually a bit more esoteric than the company's.

I try to reconcile these two totally diverse entities and keep them communicating and understanding each another and feeling good about each another. Being referee, counselor, buddy, cheerleader, and pastor are all involved in this position.

The best way I know to capsulize this is that artists are primarily idealists, and business people consider themselves pragmatists, but usually they are more like pessimists. Trying to reconcile the two is difficult because the artist is always wanting to do something that has never been done before, and the company pretty much wants to do what has already worked. So I try to balance those two worlds.

What skills that you picked up as a musician do you use today?

Everybody approaches A&R differently. Some A&R people were never musicians but are music lovers and have a real servant's attitude in doing what they do. They are there to help make things work. For me, that is definitely a prime motivation, but having been a musician, a writer, a producer, and still to some degree doing those things, I think it helps in having experiential understanding of the process. I can sit down with an artist and hear about their grievances or concerns regarding a project, their relationship with the company, or their careers. I really understand what they are saying and relate to it, and they know that. I think that helps to build a bond of trust that is really necessary not only for a good relationship between the company and the artist but for the artist to be and do his best. Artists have to have a feeling that they are understood and appreciated and that somebody is in their corner. I understand that because I've been an artist most of my adult life.

I also understand the producer's side of things because I've been there and I know what he is up against. I understand the necessities of them being on good terms with both the company and the artist. They have a responsibility to the artist to help them be the best that they can be and do the best record that they can do at that point in their career. But they also are accountable to the record company and there are certain things and considerations that they need to honor in that relationship. Sometimes if A&R doesn't have an experiential understanding of those realities, they can tend to put the producer in an uncomfortable position by making demands on him. Even though it is not a malicious thing, those demands could tend to jeopardize a real tender relationship with the artist. The artist has to be kept in a positive and creative place when working on a record. They don't need more pressure.

What would you tell someone who has aspirations to be an A&R person at a record company? How do they get in the door? What do they need to learn?

The first thing I would say is to make absolutely certain you are not doing it just because you think it would be cool to be in the record business. There are great people in the business, but a great tragedy that I have seen is people who want to climb this ladder to get close to a certain lifestyle or close to a certain group of people. That's the wrong reason to do it. If you are not going to do it to help artists to get their visions out before the people, don't do it, because at some point your motivations are going to cause your actions to get screwy. If you are doing it for the wrong reasons you are not going to do anybody any good.

So be prepared with the right kind of motives. Be willing to start in the mailroom, running tape copies, or whatever you have to do. Our CEO started as a phone salesman, which is pretty close to the mailroom. Be teachable and learn all you can. Listen to people.

I would really love to see people with a more solid musical background aspire to learn more of the business side of things as they progress in their careers. There is nothing wrong with making a change from artist, writer, or producer.

I didn't start out in high school saying I wanted to be a record executive, but there is nothing wrong with that. Back then I thought that was not cool, but the two aren't mutually exclusive. The music business needs more music people in executive positions.

Any differences between what you do here at a Christian record company and other record companies?

No, other than what we do is based on a Christian world view, which obviously impacts our motives and our methods. The mechanics are really no different, and I am finding that because we are a smaller industry, it necessitates our working harder and being more efficient. People wear more hats. I think that I am a better A&R person because I have to work harder at more things. I don't have as much help. I don't have as big a department as A&R at Capitol or MCA or EMI, so there are not as many people to bear the load. Hence, you end up doing more stuff and learning more.

What are your views about studying the business in school?

Education is a good thing, but the danger is in assuming that all you need is an education, then you are going to get a job and proceed with your game plan. The reality of it is that you can only learn so much in an academic environment. You learn more in the music business by doing than you'll ever learn by theory. It is experience that makes a difference. It is the school of hard knocks. You really oftentimes have to unlearn some of the things you learned in school. Go to school, but approach it with some real world-based wisdom and know that when you get out of school that you may still have to start in the mailroom, and that a lot of the stuff you learned doesn't really amount to a hill of beans. It is different in the real world.

◌ *RECORD PROMOTER*

The primary function of a record promoter is to encourage radio stations to play the recordings that are being released by your employer. You can either be an independent promoter, working for several artists at a time, or an in-house promoter for a record label, promoting only their artists. A record promoter spends hours on the telephone talking with people at radio stations. The job also involves attending concerts in your area and representing the label and artist to the various radio personalities that attend. You may be required to place advertising in trade papers to hype a record or arrange for other forms of media coverage.

This job is for a "people person" because it requires a likeable personality, the ability to interact with others, and the power of persuasion. You can become a record promoter by starting at the bottom with a record company. If you have a gift for interaction with people, there is a good chance you will be promoted. In-house promoters are paid a fixed salary. Independent promoters are paid a negotiable fee for each week they are "working" a record. This income can be lucrative if someone is promoting several records at a time.

Interview with Gerrie McDowell Lowdermilk
Independent Record Promoter

Gerrie has been on the inside of the record business for the last 20 years and has made a full circle. Starting as an independent promotion person in 1970, she worked her way up to become a national country sales director for Capitol Records. She is once again an independent record promoter working with most of the major labels and some of the hottest acts in country music.

Describe what you do.

I assist the record companies who hire me to work a particular record. They call me and tell me that they have a record by so-and-so and ask if I can work it. I don't like to work a lot of records; I just work enough so they won't interfere with each other. When they say the record ships on a certain date, that is when I begin to work it, and I follow it all the way to the end. I assist the labels and work with their regional representatives to get airplay.

How do you get radio stations to play someone's record?

Number one, it's the product, and it's what it is up against. In the studio, you may say you have a smash, and the record company may say that they have a smash, and granted, you may very well have a smash until it gets in the stack with all the other records. Does it compare to what else is out there? You have to convince the radio stations that it does.

There are a handful of radio stations that we call our starter stations, that don't have a limited play list. You start from there with those starter stations, and make sure they can get this record played. You have to be consistent. Call them every week and give them the information. If it's a new artist, you tell them what this artist is about, what they've done, where they're from, and any other information that they can use. If it's an artist that they've known like a Kenny Rogers or a Dolly Parton, they pretty well know these things already. Thank God it's all come down to great songs now. Name value helps but if the song is not there, the name is not going to help.

63

If a song is so great, then why employ your services?

Because every label has got a record out at the same time. It's better the more radio hears about it. The label's regional promoter from the Southwest calls about it and then an independent calls about it. It's like, "Well, maybe the label is behind this person. They are really for this record." We've got radio stations that are strictly country, your "traditionals," and then we have those with a more contemporary sound and it has to fit in their format. It's hard to explain how you get them to play it. You're a sales person. At first you're doing cold calls, but after a while you know these people and you get a sixth sense about what they'll play and what they won't, and what's going to fit their format.

You must spend hours on the phone each day.

Each day, I'm in here usually before 8 o'clock and I'm out of here at 5, 6 or 7 o'clock at night. My whole day is spent on the phone on Mondays, Tuesdays, and Wednesdays, especially. I call 220-some-odd stations a week. So on Monday and Tuesday, on which I make the bulk of the calls, I may make 40 to 90 calls in one day. I have 3x5 cards filed by day and by time, and if I can't get them I just keep trying. Our telephone bills are horrendous.

How do you know if you are making any progress?

We track these stations, too. Each station has a play list, and you ask these stations each week and find out where the record that you are working is on their chart. We work in rotation, light, medium, and heavy, so if it's at 10 or 12, it's in heavy. We have a tracking sheet and we put the numbers on there and tally everything up.

I love the word "insurance," because that is what we are, insurance for the labels to make sure that their act gets on the charts and is moved up the charts. Once you get a record added to a radio station, you don't forget it, you have to maintain it and you have to work it up their chart.

Which trades do you report to?

I work the radio stations that give their play list to the *Gavin Report* and I do have some stations that report to *R&R*. *R&R* is really your major trade magazine and *Gavin* is your secondary because we don't have *Billboard* like we used to. Some stations overlap, reporting to all three, but *Billboard* is computerized and now they put some kind of little computer box in a city that monitors the radio stations and what they are playing. So the personal touch is gone. Consequently, that is why everybody has transferred everything over to *R&R* and *Gavin*.

How did you get started?

I started out at a radio station in high school and actually started as a switchboard operator at a station in Dallas. On the weekends I worked what they called traffic, or continuity, and even did some on-the-air work, doing some spots and stuff like that. I went to college and never considered getting into the business.

I moved to Los Angeles and my husband at that time was at radio station KHJ so I really got to see a lot of the workings. Bill Drayco was like the programmer then. The record companies not only worked the music director and program director, but the on-air jocks as well, because they could pick what they wanted to play back then. I worked at a motion picture sound company, so I knew a lot about sound and got to meet a lot of people. Between these two businesses I saw that this is where I wanted to be.

I moved back to Dallas after a divorce, and someone knowing my background said they knew an independent promoter named Ernie Fellows who needed someone to work for him. He hired me. He would work the pop stations and I would work the black and country stations. I stayed with him for a couple of years.

Then Polygram (then they were called Mercury) needed someone to come in and work with them and that is how it all started.

Is there any difference between working country stations and working pop stations?

It's basically the same, with as much pressure in either marketplace.

Do you ever have personal contact with the people you call? Do you go on the road?

I worked for Capitol for 13 years and yes, that was my job. I would go to the radio stations, make personal contact with these people, take them to dinner, get acquainted, get to know their format and what their interests were. Another part of the job was to be at the shows for the artists that are signed to a label. You make sure that radio stations meet the artists whose records they are playing. It's the personal touch in our business. With a newer act, we would take the artist to the radio station so they could do an interview or give autographs. This is very important, because radio is our avenue to reach the people so we can sell records, and that's what this business is all about.

Is there any training ground for this occupation or any school you can go to?

You can go to school but you don't ever get the training till you are out there doing it and knowing what it's all about. Here in Nashville, record companies use interns from colleges. They aren't paid, but they may be in the publicity department or the promotion department so they get a good feel as to what is going on in the music business. This town is really excellent for young people that are interested.

Are there any special talents that you should have?

The gift of gab. You can't be afraid. You've got to be a salesman and you have to sell yourself, too. You've got a record that you want played, but you're really selling yourself.

<u>ON TOUR</u>

Concert Promoter, Booking Agent, Road Manager,
Tour Accountant, Road Crew/Technical,
and Merchandising

A successful road tour encompasses much more than artists and musicians; it depends upon many, many support people. This section is devoted to career opportunities associated with touring: promoter, booking agent, road manager, tour accountant, road crew/technical crew, and merchandising.

During my touring years with Kenny Rogers, we averaged 180 touring days a year. There were seven of us when we first started out: Kenny, five musicians, and a road manager who did everything from driving the equipment truck to running sound and lights. More musicians and support personnel were added over the years as Kenny's popularity grew. We had as many as 50 people traveling with the entourage during the peak years, which still paled in comparison to the Michael Jackson or Rolling Stones tours that numbered well over 100 persons. In recent years, Kenny's entourage has leveled out at around 20 people who travel full time with the Kenny Rogers tour. They include:

- Road manager
- Eight musicians
- Production manager/keyboard tech
- Equipment manager
- Front-of-house mixer
- Monitor mixer/audio tech
- Lighting director
- Coach drivers
- Truck drivers
- Wardrobe/dressing room person
- Rigger

When there are special events or changes in the show, the numbers occasionally swell to include management, a lighting designer, show producer, publicity person, or additional technical people.

CONCERT PROMOTER

A promoter does just what the name implies by bringing an artist to a given location and promoting the show. The promoter has to be familiar with how well an artist will do in a particular region. For example, some country artists will be very successful in Dallas but not in New York City. This is for the obvious reason that country music is more popular in Texas than in New York. A promoter has to be familiar with the local media (TV, radio, newspapers) and how to use them to promote and advertise an upcoming show. A promoter gets people excited about buying a ticket to see an artist perform. The promoter must be aware of the artist's stage, lighting, sound, and dressing room requirements (these are usually stated in the artist's contract). The promoter is responsible for securing a building and negotiating a fee for its use. Sometimes this includes procuring security people and liability insurance, but more often, these items are part of the building package.

You need a substantial amount of money to start out in this business. The promoter usually pays the up-front costs for the concert, including the price of the act, which can be considerable. Tickets are sold and the promoter keeps what is left after expenses. This can be a great deal of money if ticket sales are good, but it can represent a huge loss if ticket sales are poor. Many amateurs (myself included) have lost money trying to promote concerts. Just because *you* think an act will do well in a certain city does not mean that the ticket-buying public will agree with you. A successful promoter must be very knowledgeable about the music business and have experience marketing the product, in this case a concert.

You can start in the promoting business by hooking up with a rock and roll band in high school or college and promoting school dances. From there to the big time is a long, hard road, and I recommend obtaining a college degree, preferably in business management or marketing. Journalism skills are also helpful since the promoter spends much time dealing with the media. Good negotiating skills are a necessity.

I also believe there is something to be said for the God-given ability to sell, which in essence, is what a promoter does. *Pollstar* Magazine (http://www. pollstar.com) is a weekly publication serving the concert promotion industry. It is widely read by people in the business end of music and its pages contain much valuable information for both the novice and the pro.

One last word of caution: Many fortunes have been made and lost in this business. Do your homework well before jumping into it.

BOOKING AGENT

A booking agent is responsible for "selling" acts to the promoters and other talent buyers. The job of a well-known agent with a well-known booking agency often consists of waiting for the telephone to ring with requests to book artists that agent represents. However, it takes hard work to become a well-known booking agent. It means spending hours on end calling prospective talent buyers. This includes everyone from the person handling the Asparagus Festival in Hart, Michigan, to a promoter who wants to take an act into Carnegie Hall. A solid knowledge of demographics is required. For example, a booking agent worth his or her salt wouldn't attempt to sell an act like Usher to the Houston Rodeo.

A booking agent always tries to match the audience with the act and vice versa. Sales abilities are an absolute necessity. The agent must also be able to maintain good relationships with management, press, record companies, and the artist.

Booking agents earn a percentage of whatever money they get for their acts, usually 10 to 15 percent of the gross. An agent who works with a large agency must split this commission with the company. If that agency is handling acts that sell in the $25,000- to $50,000-per-night range, there is plenty of money to go around.

You can get started as a booking agent by becoming a receptionist and working your way up the ladder. Many agents are former road musicians that got tired of traveling but wanted to stay in the business. Others may come from telemarketing backgrounds.

Interview with Bobby Roberts
Booking Agent

Bobby was initially a musician, but his business acumen led him to national status as a manager and talent agent. As a manager, his roster has included Mark Farner, John Anderson, and Paul Overstreet. His booking agency handles many major country and rock acts in worldwide markets.

69

What does a booking agent do?

A booking agency is very similar to an employment agency. We find work for artists, musicians, or entertainers. That can be a fair, a festival, a nightclub, Las Vegas, a European tour, concert halls, theaters, and so on. We put a buyer and a seller together. The artist is the seller with his talent that he has to sell in the marketplace. The talent buyer is the one who will contract with us to bring in a particular artist. We get an offer from the buyer and we take that to the artist or the artist's manager, and they will decide at that point whether they want to take that engagement. If they do, then we go back and issue all the contracts and do all the due diligence work up to the date of the performance. We are monitoring the deposits, getting the paperwork done, and communicating with all the parties involved.

What skills do you have to have to do this job?

Most important, you have to have very strong telemarketing skills because 95 percent of your time is spent on the phone with people that have never met you. You have to have a personable phone voice, a sales-oriented personality, and a lot of tenacity.

How did you get started in this business?

We had our own band back in Michigan and we had a certain amount of success on a regional basis playing a rotation of clubs in Michigan. We ran our band like a business. We did our own booking, and I usually handled all of that for the group, communicating with the club owners, then negotiating the deal and so forth. After I did that for a few years, we gained a certain reputation. Some of my musician friends asked me if I would help them get into a nightclub because they didn't have the wherewithal and the personality to sell their own act. After I did that a couple of times, the light bulb went on and I said to myself, "Hey, I ought to be a booking agent." That is what I did. I helped some of my friends get into places and I charged them 10 percent. I started my first booking agency in 1974.

How does one learn to be a booking agent?

There are regional booking agencies in every state in the country, and you can go there and try to find yourself a job in a situation like that. If you feel you have a knack for it, do it on a regional level and learn how to go about soliciting the dates and closing the deals.

The key to any successful salesperson, whether they are booking entertainers or selling cars, is whether they can close the sale. That is where the real art comes in. You can learn that by working for a regional agency. If you have the confidence, you can come to a town like Nashville, Los Angeles, or New York and visit the different booking agencies. Agencies are always looking for an energetic person with the type of personality that would make a good agent. Even though we are not always hiring, we are always keeping our eyes and ears open for a good agent.

I have two young guys that just started working with me, one of which is probably going to make it and the other one won't. The first young guy has closing skills. I like to have a new agent observe one of our veteran agents to see what a typical business day is like and how different situations are handled. We give the new agent an orientation to the business and the opportunity to ask questions. Then we give them a territory and some sales leads. Within a matter of six weeks the one guy was nailing the dates down and doing very well. The other fellow just isn't closing. You can develop this to a certain degree but you either have it or you don't for closing sales. Not everybody is meant to be a salesperson; their talent may lie elsewhere.

Do you think having a musical background is helpful?

I certainly do, and I think one thing that has helped our company grow is the fact that we do understand the problems on the road. We understand routing, food, and what it's like to be on stage because most of us at our company made our living as entertainers at one time or another. I think it is a big advantage as far as setting the rapport with the artists themselves.

Do you feel a college education is necessary?

No, I don't believe it is necessary, but I want to say that with this thought in mind: I spent five years in college and I think it helped focus me. College helps us find our niche and what our areas of expertise might be. I took marketing in college and found that I really got into sales. I really zeroed in and studied marketing and sales and I think that has helped me tremendously, but I don't think it is a necessity to be a successful agent. I think it is good to go to college because it helps set the tone for the rest of your life.

How does the booking agent make his money?

As a business we generate a 10–20 percent commission off the engagement, most of the time 10 percent. There are certain occasions where we derive a higher commission. (That commission will be off the gross amount of the contract price.) If you have an artist booked for $10,000, the agency makes $1,000. Now agents are paid generally a salary or draw, plus commission, which gives them the added incentive. Some agents can earn well into six figures, $200,000–250,000 a year personal income. Some agents earn $12,000 a year. Again it is how well you do your job. If you are doing well, people notice that. Then you are going to get opportunities either at other companies or you may develop your own company. Possibilities are numerous. The Jim Halsey Company, a very large country booking agency, was netting several million dollars a year.

Rosters are a very important part of it. Jim Halsey Company had a very strong roster of superstars. Consequently, his income was much higher than most. It takes the same amount of time and sometimes less time to book a superstar than someone who is working for $3,000 a night. The process is exactly the same; the difference is the amount of zeroes on the end of your commission.

◯ *ROAD MANAGER*

The road manager oversees and coordinates the day-to-day operations of a tour. Duties may include getting the group from point A to point B, paying the bills, serving as liaison between the artist and the press and between the artist and the fans, and crisis resolution. If something comes up that needs to be done, the road manager will usually be the one to do it, thereby earning a reputation as being the most overworked person on tour.

The road manager normally deals with the artist and musicians as opposed to dealing with the road crew and technical people. (The production manager usually handles them.)

Average pay would be around $200 a day; however, salaries vary considerably, depending on the size of the act and the responsibilities involved. The job can easily be a springboard from which to launch a career in artist management or concert promotion.

An even temperament and affable personality are almost mandatory because the road manger interacts with many personalities on the road and usually takes the heat when anything goes wrong. Short courses in conflict management, which are offered through colleges and private consulting firms, are becoming increasingly popular with business people. It would be wise for anyone hoping to become a road manager to take one of these seminars. One very effective road manager that I know worked with emotionally disturbed children before his entry into the music business!

Some road managers start in T-shirt sales or as sluggers (stage hands) on a tour. Others start at the bottom in management companies, and as their skills improve, they are assigned to various acts the company represents. A music background is not necessary but is helpful when dealing with artists and their egos.

Interview with Pat McCollum
Tour Manager for Kenny G.

Pat started as a custom coach-builder and worked his way up to road manager for one of the hottest acts in the jazz/pop arena. Here he shares his insights on what he does and how he got there.

What does your job involve?
It includes setting up all the projects (for each city and venue that we go to on tour), such as arranging radio and TV interviews for Kenny, meeting with local dignitaries, and, in general, just making sure the show goes off as planned. Most of the in-house duties belong to the production manager. I don't arrive at the venue till maybe an hour or so before the show, and when the show is over we leave. Essentially my job is "personalizing" with Kenny.

How did you get into this?
I knew C.K. Spurlock (Kenny Rogers' promoter) and another guy who built tour coaches for Kenny. I helped build those coaches, then I built coaches for the group Alabama. When I wasn't building, I was driving them so I learned the ins and outs of being on the road. I got hired as a driver in 1987 by Kenny G. In 1989, Kenny's tour manager left and I was hired to replace him. I learned about road managing from our former manager whom I worked closely with.

What advice do you have for someone coming out of high school that wants to do what you do?
Well, one thing I learned a long time ago is that if you are not in Nashville or Los Angeles or maybe New York (not as much anymore), you should get there. I tell people that all over the country who ask that very question.

College is not necessary. You really learn from being out there and doing whatever it takes. Work hard and keep yourself straight and clean.

What can a road manager expect to make?
Between $50,000 and $100,000 depending on, of course, how much you are working. You may be on a flat retainer for weeks off and then a larger sum for weeks traveled. This seems most common. Some of the bigger acts pay a straight salary. You can make a good living even if you get a retainer and only work part of the year. I also have something to fall back on with my coach-building business.

What does a bus driver make?
They make about $1,000 a week but they work seven days a week and every week of the year.

◯ *TOUR ACCOUNTANT/MONEY MANAGEMENT*

Just as in any other business, the music business has financial matters that must be dealt with. Accountants who have little or no music business training may handle touring financial services. However, many acts carry a specialized tour accountant with music business experience who handles all monetary transactions on the road, from dishing out band and crew per diems to counting box office receipts.

You can train for this position by taking business and accounting courses as well as some music business courses that are offered at a few schools around the country. After that, it is a matter of gaining experience. You can start out as a "gopher" for a record company or concert promoter. T-shirt sales also are a good starting place since it involves handling money. A music background isn't a necessity, but I believe a love for the business and a desire to tour would be prerequisites. Why else would anyone in their right mind want to count money on the road for days and weeks on end?

Interview with Glen Grabski
Tour Accountant for Kenny Rogers

Though never a professional musician, Glen's love for music led him to pursue a career in the administrative end of the business. Besides being a tour accountant, he has experience in concert production, promotion, and artist management. An admitted audiophile, Glen can get real serious when it comes to talking about the blues.

What is your background?
I was a promoter with Feyline Presents, Denver. For the last three years I have worked with Kenny Rogers and also have done some work with 38 Special.

What is your daily routine?
I spend a couple of hours on the phone advancing shows, working on upcoming shows. I get caught up with the office and make sure that our accounts are current. I spend a couple of hours on my computer catching up on my paperwork, petty cash, and show settlements. In the afternoon I can usually take some personal time. Around 3 to 4 o'clock, my business day really

starts. I check out the seating and the way they take tickets. I look at the number of entrances to the hall. I talk to the production manager about any unique problems that day that might cost us more money. By the time the show starts, I have done a lot of work.

I have walked the halls and made sure T-shirts are being merchandised correctly. I have made sure the ticket takers are handling tickets correctly and no long lines are forming at the doors to delay the beginning of the show. During the show I am in the box office or the hall manager's office starting the settlement procedure. I finish my day about an hour after the show has finished.

How did you get your start in this business?

It started my freshman year in college at the University of Arizona. I had a friend who was working with the college concert department. I started hanging posters and going around to spread the word on our shows. I also worked security at concerts, worked in the box office, and ended up running the box office. Later I became production manager for a year, and after that I headed up all advertising and promotion. I stayed on for my fifth year of college, graduate work, and at that point I was running the college concert program. I handled booking and contract negotiations and was running the campus concert program.

With this experience I got hired right out of school by Feyline to work at Starlight Amphitheater in Kansas City. Basically I did advertising and pro-motion, but I also "settled" the shows; that is, I went over the financial numbers every night. I enjoyed this part the most and in time became one of two reps for Feyline that worked out-of-state shows. I traveled a lot promoting and settling shows west of the Mississippi River.

Do you have a background in music?

No, not really. As a kid I messed around with it, and I did work in a record store where I would spend hours reading backs of record albums and listening. Music was more than a hobby for me. I have an extensive record collection. I am an audiophile, always listening to the stereo.

What sort of college background prepared you for what you are doing?

My education majors are finance and business economics with a strong minor in accounting. Even with my college degree, the experience working in the field during college gave me more of a background than I feel any educational system could. There are people out there now doing my job who don't have degrees.

75

There seem to be many people coming out of college who see tour accounting as a very fascinating part of the business to get into.

Does every major act have a tour accountant?

Yes, any major tour does have one. When I was out with 38 Special as tour manager, I also acted as tour accountant. That tour did not warrant having a separate accountant. Really major tours have two or three accountants, with a head accountant and his assistant and a separate merchandise accountant.

What can a tour accountant or someone who does similar work expect to make?

Most tour accountants work with rock and roll and they make between $1,500 and $2,500 a week, depending on the act and his responsibilities. There are some jobs paying $750 to $1,000 a week range. The average would be $1,500 to $1,700 a week.

What advice would you give a young person wanting to get into this field?

It is not a job that you can ever apply for, it's a job that you work for. It is true that it is "who you know" but it's also "what you know." Absorb as much as you can, listen to everyone, and play it straight. Be on the up and up with everyone and learn as you go.

ROAD CREW/MUSICAL TECHNICIAN

Qualifications for this job used to be a strong back and a weak mind because the primary function of the "roadie" was to unload, set up, and tear down band equipment. However, the technological advances in musical instruments, sound reinforcement, and lighting have changed the job qualifications considerably. Knowledge of electronics is a must, as is a good amount of computer expertise. Some of the larger touring acts employ full-time musician/programmers who are responsible for maintaining all the computer-based instruments. If one of these instruments goes down, chances are it can't be fixed with a screwdriver and duct tape. It is a job for someone with an electronics degree or, at the very least, someone with a lot of practical electronic experience. Stage hands (sluggers) do most of the heavy work, but the operation and maintenance of the high-tech musical gear is the responsibility of the road crew.

Crewmembers usually hire out on a daily or weekly basis with salaries ranging from $400 to $1,000 a week. You can start out by unloading trucks at the local municipal auditorium and learn as you go, or you can send your resume to any of the sound reinforcement companies across the United States.

They might be interested if you have practical experience with electronics and/or sound reinforcement.

Interview with Mike Wolpert
Production Manager/Head Technician for Kenny Rogers

What Mike didn't say in the following interview was that he is a talented keyboard player as well as a technical whiz. When we had unexpected absences, Mike served as "relief keyboardist," rising to the occasion on a moment's notice!

How did you get your training?

It started in grade school, tinkering around with electronics and being a keyboard player. I'd hook up boxes with speakers in them to stereos and that is where I got my interest.

Our high school offered electronics courses and the basic electronic course helped me with my tinkering a little bit. Of course, that was before the arrival of the digital technology that is prevalent today. Back then it was all analog, so we got the basic knowledge about tubes and things like that. We grew up with computer technology as it came out.

After high school I got a job with Claire Brothers Audio Company because I played in a band that they did sound for. (Claire Brothers of Lititz, Penn., is the major sound company in the United States, providing audio services for many high-visibility acts such as Kenny Rogers, Elton John, etc.) Even before the band split up, we were already learning how to fix things and had the chance to learn the latest technology gear during this time.

How does Claire Brothers go about hiring people?

Claire Brothers has their own system of doing things. They would hire several college-educated people, PhDs who would do their research and development and train others. Equipment sent out from Claire was top-notch, well-tested.

Someone without a degree would need to send a resume. It is good to have some kind of background in what you are wanting to get into. For example, some teens will work as a disc jockey at a radio station to get experience with equipment, mixing, etc. Some run sound for a local band so they learn about mixing, monitors, feedback, and all that sort of stuff. The resume does help. It also really helps to have a good recommendation from someone in the business that says you are a very good worker. An employer will take note of a good worker over just a "brain" or a genius. Most of it is dedication to the job. Then they hire for a trial period.

77

When I first got started I didn't even go out on the road for a year or longer. During that time I worked in the wood shop and learned the theory and electronics behind building speakers. One day, the boss walked in and said that he needed someone to mix for Diana Ross. He pointed to me and said, "You're the guy." I went out and learned how to do monitors for her. That's how it began on the road for me.

How did you get the job as Kenny Rogers' production manager?

In between our shows for Claire Brothers, I would work on Kenny shows. Kenny had old keyboard gear then and when it needed repairing they would send it off. While on the road with Kenny after I finished my monitor work, I started repairing the equipment. One day he came up to me and asked me if I wanted a job.

Who else have you worked for?

I've worked for Stevie Nicks, Bruce Springsteen, The Grateful Dead, Rolling Stones, J. Giles Band – always mixing monitors.

Have you ever mixed mains (main speakers)?

I never wanted to mix mains because I always thought that the monitor mixing was the most exciting. You become part of the band because if they don't hear correctly the show is not going to be right. You get closer to your artist than the house (mixing) guy, in my opinion. Many times the artist knows the monitor man by name but he won't even know the house guy.

What would you advise someone wanting to get into the business as a crew member or a technician?

You should go out and get as much literature on some of these new devices as possible. We grew up with the technology, but nowadays you're stepping right into it and digital technology is well beyond what it was when it was first introduced. Learn the gear and the principles behind what you are going to be working with. For example, you have to know what a diode does, what a cathode does, what a flip-flip circuit is. You have to know your basic electronics to be able to make stuff work.

Also, keep your (criminal) record clean because if you have to go out of the country on a tour, you won't be able to go if you have a record. I know guys who have been fired for that reason.

Is there any place you recommend to go to learn electronics?

Stay in school! Many people think you have to go to college but vo-tech training can be part of your high school education. It gives you a three-year course in electronics. You'll know almost as much coming out of those courses as you would four years of college. They are giving you a jump on everybody else who is going to college for electrical engineering.

What kind of money can somebody make with a company like Claire Brothers Audio?

After you are there for a while as a monitor mixer or crew technician, you can make $100,000 or more per year. The guy that took my job when I left Claire Brothers made $140,000 the previous year with Bruce Springsteen. When I was with Claire Brothers, I regularly got bonuses from $12,000 to $14,000 a year from different acts.

Do they still hire "roadies"?

Yes, they call them "sluggers" when they first start. If they are willing to learn, that can grow into another position. Like any other vocation, touring companies look for people who are willing to work hard and you will advance if you do work hard. These people can make $20,000 to $30,000 a year starting.

MERCHANDISING/T-SHIRT PEOPLE

Selling merchandise is an important part of concert promotion. Don't think this isn't big business! It isn't uncommon for a popular act to earn thousands a night in T-shirt and other merchandise sales. It might not sound very glamorous to an aspiring musician, but it's a good starting place for someone who wants to break into management or promotion. Kenny Rogers' road manager, Gene Roy, started out by selling T-shirts. As his familiarity with the business grew, he worked his way into other areas of the tour and was eventually promoted to road manager. Now he's in charge of just about everything on the road.

There are companies that specialize in merchandising for recording artists. Winterland is one such company. They pay the artist a fee up front for the right to sell merchandise with that artist's name, logo, or likeness on it.

It is no longer possible, as it once was, to go into a building, sell T-shirts, and take the money out in a brown paper bag. The building management usually wants a percentage of the sales and sometimes they insist on their own people selling the merchandise. It varies from town to town and building to building. The people who sell the merchandise usually earn a 10 percent commission on their gross sales.

Interview with Mark Apple
Owner, Backstreet

At the time of this interview, Mark owned and operated his own independent merchandising company, Backstreet. His clientele included Don Williams and several Christian artists including Steven Curtis Chapman, White Heart, Jeff Moore, Charlie Peacock, Out Of The Grey, Susan Ashton, and Wes King. He has a lot of enthusiasm for his profession and is proof that you don't have to be in the band to be in the business.

Tell me about your background and how you got started in this.

I went to college at Anderson University in Indiana to study Music Business. That's where Bill Gaither and Sandi Patti are from, and because of their success they have put much into the music program. There I met Stephen Curtis Chapman, now a pretty successful Christian artist. We were in a band together for a couple of years there; I played keyboards. We traveled the summers and represented the school. When I was a freshman I met Scott Troxel who works for Blanton/Harrell who lives here in Nashville. He worked on Amy Grant's tour, taking care of the merchandise. We both graduated the same time. The next day he needed an assistant on Amy Grant's Unguarded tour in '85. That's how I got involved in merchandising. I was his assistant when he was the manager.

What exactly do you do as a merchandiser, and how does this all work?

Backstreet, the company that we own, buys shirts from the mills. Then we contract out printers here in town to do the printing. Some artists purchase the finished product from us. They take care of selling it and we have nothing to do with it once they buy it from us. With others, we do not sell the product to them. We retain the ownership of the product and we are responsible for selling it at the concerts. Then we give the artists a monthly royalty statement based on the sales.

Besides being on the artist end of selling merchandise, I've worked at Starwood Amphitheater since it opened up, with a crew here in town. We sell merchandise that the various groups bring in. They pay a percentage to Starwood and to the company that is in charge of the vending there, and we are paid a percentage for selling. Approximately 4 percent of all the sales is split up between all of the sellers. So if there are 10 sellers, then the 4 percent is split between the 10.

What sort of training do you need for this?

I don't think there is any specific training. I ended up getting my degree in marketing. At the time I was not planning on doing any of this but it ended up working out perfectly. I have a double major in Music Business and Marketing. I don't want to say that you have to have that sort of background to get into this, because there are really no requirements at all.

What would you tell a young person interested in getting into this business? Where does one start?

I would say at the local venues, try to get on the shows that come into town. Whether it is at the theater or an arena, try to find out through the management of the building who is in charge of hiring and try to get a job that way. Then if you are interested in going on tour you can meet some of the people that come in, some of the road managers, some of the bands. Find out from them or from the merchandising companies who their agents are and try to build up contacts with them.

Who are you doing merchandising for right now?

I work with Don Williams, Steven Curtis Chapman, White Heart, Little Texas (they are a new country band on Warner Bros.), Jeff Moore, Charlie Peacock, Out of the Grey, Susan Ashton, and Wes King. Most of these are Christian artists. We have a few country artists that we are talking to about '92, but I guess I shouldn't mention anything in case things don't work out.

TAKING CARE OF BUSINESS
Artist Management, Music Attorney, and Publicist

I have placed these three positions in a separate category because they encompass all aspects of the music business. Management, legal and publicity people are involved *everywhere*, from working with individual songwriters to handling large concert tours. The following job descriptions and interviews will give you a glimpse into the working lives of the people who walk in these footsteps.

◯ *ARTIST MANAGEMENT*

A manager is responsible for guiding an artist's career. It is helpful (but not necessary) that a manager have musical abilities and perhaps some experience as a performer.

A manager makes business and career decisions, negotiates record contracts, and negotiates fees for the artist's TV and personal appearances. It is essential that a manager have expertise in dealing with people. Good salesmanship is a plus. After all, a manager has to "sell" the artist.

A manager takes a percentage of the artist's income as payment for services. This percentage can be as little as 10 to 15 percent or, as in the case of Colonel Tom Parker (the late Elvis Presley's manager) as high as 50 percent! Income is based on how well the job is done. An artist may have all the talent in the world but not be successful without the marketing skills of a good manager. Many careers have been "made" by astute management.

A lot of managers I know started out as musicians and came up through the ranks. Others broke in by just hanging out with bands they liked, doing menial tasks, perhaps moving up to road manager and eventually achieving the status of manager. A college degree is not mandatory but certainly helpful. There are a lot of big guns out there with backgrounds from Harvard Business School, and like the old saying goes, you have to be able to swim with the sharks. *Billboard* magazine publishes guides for management and booking agents at various times of the year. These books are helpful to a prospective manager, as is *This Business of Music* and the weekly *Pollstar Magazine.*

Interview with Ken Kragen
Artist Manager

Ken's artist roster has included some of the most celebrated names in the music business. A giant in the industry, he has shared his knowledge by means of national seminars and college courses at UCLA, and a book titled Life Is A Contact Sport.

What does it take to be a manager?

Anyone can be a manager. All it takes is the consent of a performer, artist, or actor to say, "This person is going to represent me to the other people that I have to deal with." As a result, managers have come from every conceivable direction. Wives or husbands are very often managers, in fact, many times without any previous skill or ability. So are lawyers, publicists, former musicians who have the business and executive skills to manage. For example, Peter Asher, (of Peter & Gordon, a group from the '60s) became a major manager by using his musical ability. He is a manager/producer, producing recordings for Linda Ronstadt, James Taylor, and a number of others. He was first a producer and then became a manager also.

Agents, record company executives, promoters – all have become managers. There is no specific training for a manager. However, Middle Tennessee State University offers a management course, as does SMU in Dallas and Northwestern University in Chicago. There also are extension courses on management skills taught at UCLA and USC.

Another important thing is to clearly define the difference between a manager and an agent. An agent basically books work, but in Tennessee, an agent can be a manager. In California you can't be both. I don't know about other states. The agent's job is to secure employment for the artist and specifically deal with buyers in all the different fields: television, motion pictures, and personal appearances. Then the agent submits those jobs to the client or to his selected representative. So the manager handles business between the artist and the agent. In Kenny Rogers' case, C.K. Spurlock acts as his agent. In California a manager is technically not supposed to negotiate employment, but any good manager is soliciting and trying to get employment, negotiating in tandem with an agent or attorney creating the activity. My definition of the manager's role is to do everything but sing.

I do anything and everything to further the artist's career, whether that is suggesting a piece of wardrobe, working with a publicist on a story, working with an agent on a booking, producing a television project, seeing that my clients have good money management, or seeing that there is proper legal representation. Whatever it takes to enhance the full spectrum of the career.

A manager is much like the chief operating officer of a corporation in which the artist is both the owner and the product. The manager controls all the various "divisions" whose job it is to properly create and sell that product: manufacturing, i.e. the record company or television company; sales, i.e. the agent; communications or publicity, i.e. the publicist; legal, just like in a regular corporation. The manager's job is to see that those roles are filled by competent people, that they all do their jobs enthusiastically and work well for the artist.

The artist, at the same time, has the final say. His career is the corporation's major asset and ultimately it is his (or her) life that is the most affected. The manager is not generally "employed" by the artist's company, in that he usually has his own business.

The background of people who come to management and their previous roles in an artist's life before the artist is successful dictate the styles with which people manage. Some people are great negotiators, some are motivators or cheerleaders, some are creative managers who come up with creative ideas. Some managers are record producers like Peter Asher. There's a broad spectrum. Some managers are simply glorified road managers. In those cases, the artist runs his own career and the managers just service his needs. As varied as the backgrounds of managers are, so are the styles and roles of the managers. This is not a business that has a lot of rules.

What is your background?

In high school and college, I promoted concerts. As I was coming out of Harvard Business School, I was asked to be executive secretary for a group called the Limelighters. I did one of the most gutsy things I've ever done in my life. I told them that I didn't go to Harvard Business School to be someone's executive secretary, but if they wanted a manager to let me know. Later I got a letter asking me to be their manager, but at the time I was still in school so I told them they had to wait six months until I graduated. So I worked for the Limelighters and went to school at the same time. I came out of school to manage, but with no knowledge about what management was or how to do it. I learned from them, and from my own mistakes, and I built a career around it.

84

Who have you managed in your career?

I started by producing the very first Kingston Trio concert ever and then managed the Limelighters. The day the Limelighters broke up, I signed the Smothers Brothers who I managed through the '60s. Through their show, I picked up a series of artists, Mason Williams, John Hartford, Bob Einstein who later became "Super Dave," Jennifer Warnes, Pat Paulsen. Through the Smothers Brothers lawyers I found the First Edition (later Kenny Rogers and the First Edition), Lionel Richie, Kim Carnes, J. Giles Band, Olivia Newton John and the Bee Gees. Currently I also manage a hot country newcomer, Travis Tritt, and actor Burt Reynolds.

MUSIC ATTORNEY

The music attorney handles the legal aspects of the music business, which may involve negotiating contracts, representing individuals who have breached contracts, or interpreting copyright law. The attorney also serves as a liaison between the artist or songwriter and music industry representatives. The music business abounds in contracts – record company contracts, publishing contracts, production contracts, etc. The complex legal wording is extremely difficult for a lay person to decipher. Therefore, there is a tremendous need for people who understand both the law and the music business.

A music attorney must be a law school graduate who has passed the bar. The most obvious way for an attorney or law student to get into the music business is to become a legal assistant, paralegal, intern, or junior partner with a law firm that specializes in music law. There are many such firms in Nashville, New York, and Los Angeles. Obviously, a law school student who can work part time as a paralegal or assistant will have an edge over those who have no experience before graduation.

A good source of information for the would-be music attorney is the book *This Business of Music*, published by Billboard Magazine Co. It contains examples of various types of music contracts plus an explanation of copyright law. I recommend it for anyone who is contemplating a career in music law or who simply wants to learn about the business.

Music attorneys usually charge an hourly fee for services. Sometimes the attorney is asked to present a project to a record company on behalf of an artist, in which case the attorney might work for a percentage of the deal, if he or she believes in the project. This is one way a music attorney can be involved in the creative process of making music.

Interview with Steve Winogradsky
Music Attorney

Steve Winogradsky, co-founder/partner of Winogradsky/Sobel, has more than 25 years experience as an attorney in the music industry. He and his company provide music business affairs and legal support for composers, songwriters, music publishers, recording artists, and television, film, video, and multi-media producers. They also provide music clearance and licensing in all media for several production companies and worldwide administration of the publishing catalogs for a number of clients. He has served as director of Music Business Affairs for Hanna-Barbera Productions, Inc., managing director of Music, Legal, & Business Affairs for MCA Home Entertainment, director of Music Licensing and Administration for Universal Pictures and Universal Television, and vice president of Business Affairs for The Clearing House, Ltd. He was twice elected president of the California Copyright Conference after serving for nine years on its board of directors. He also served for four years as president of The Association of Independent Music Publishers.

Steve was named an Outstanding Instructor in Entertainment Studies and Performing Arts at UCLA Extension, where he has taught since 1997. He has written numerous magazine articles on the subject of music for motion pictures and television and has lectured extensively on a variety of music-related topics.

In addition, Steve is a guitarist, singer, and songwriter, and is both a composer and publisher member of ASCAP.

Describe your typical day.

There is no set pattern to my day. Every day includes lots of e-mail and phone calls from clients and people I'm doing business with, reviewing and drafting of agreements, negotiating deals, etc. My practice is so varied that I rarely get to spend a lot of time in one specific area, which keeps it from getting boring. Plus, there are the office management issues, making sure everyone has an assignment, answering questions from staff, reviewing their work, etc.

How did you come to be a music/entertainment attorney? Did you start out as a musician?

I've been a musician since I was a kid, playing guitar from the age of 8. I played in bands during college, then worked full time as a musician after graduation. After realizing that my talent didn't match my career goals, I went back to law school and was lucky enough shortly thereafter to work for a music clearance and licensing company representing TV and film producers in obtaining the rights to music to include in their projects. After that, I became head of licensing for Universal Pictures and Television and MCA Home Entertainment. After a few years there, I got a great opportunity to be head of Music Business Affairs at Hanna-Barbera, where I was able to do a lot more than just licensing. When HB got sold, I went into private practice.

How important is it to be "musical" to do what you do?

In doing music clearance, it is not so much about being "musical" as having knowledge about the music. Growing up, I read all the liner notes on albums, so I knew who the writers and musicians were on the tracks, which helped me figure out from whom to license them.

As an attorney, my musical background doesn't really help at all in reading and negotiating deals. Where it does help is in my relationships with my clients, as I understand better than some the process of what they do and can help create deals that foster their creativity and protect their income streams.

What are the high and low points of your job?

I love dealing with clients (most of them, anyway) and the thrill of production, where deadlines make everyone work harder and, hopefully, smarter. The paperwork can be overwhelming, so that would be the bad part.

High points of my career are when I've done a great job for my clients. I think I'm pretty good at what I do, but every once in a while an opportunity comes along where I get to exercise some creativity on behalf of a client to get them a better deal than either of us thought possible when we started the negotiation. I've been lucky enough to have this happen a few times.

There haven't been too many low points, fortunately. A couple of times I've advised against a deal for a client who took it anyway and when it went sour, they blamed me. And getting laid off when Hanna-Barbera was sold was tough, although it allowed me to start my own practice, which I enjoyed.

What would you tell someone starting out who has aspirations to become an entertainment attorney?

Don't! (laughter) It's a tough field to break into because everyone wants to be in show biz. Realize that it's not about hanging with rock stars but working hard to protect your clients while having a little fun along the way. At this point in my life, not only do I not want to do anything else, I have no other skills. (more laughter)

PUBLICIST

It is not by chance that articles about recording artists appear on the Web or in newspapers and magazines. These press releases are the carefully timed efforts of the publicist, who supplies the media with whatever information the artist and/or management want to get before the public. The publicist deals with all forms of media: newspapers, magazines, radio, and television. Journalistic skills are essential, as is the ability to interact and communicate with people.

The publicist might accompany the artist on major tours to interact daily with newspapers and to arrange radio and television interviews for the artist. The publicist organizes these functions daily while simultaneously maintaining national press coverage. A concert promoter might work with the publicist to generate interest and excitement before the concert date. This effort usually translates into more ticket sales. Some management companies have their own in-house publicists but most contract with a publicity firm. Large firms, such as Rogers & Cowan, have tremendous media resources at their disposal, plus years of experience networking in the music business.

A degree in journalism and/or communications is the obvious first step for anyone hoping to become a publicist. It also would help to volunteer to be publicity chairperson for college musicals and dramas or local theater groups in order to have something more than the degree on your resume. Maintain copies of anything you write that is published so that you can send the best of the lot with your job applications.

After graduation, try to get your foot in the door with a publicity firm – at whatever level is offered.

Interview with Cheryl Kagan
Senior Vice President, Rogers & Cowan, the Largest Independent PR Company in the World (Based in Los Angles with offices in New York, Washington, and London)

Cheryl's interview, from an editor's standpoint, pretty much wrote itself. That should come as no surprise. Her expertise in communications, charming personality, and zest for her work have propelled her to the top. Since this interview in 1993, Cheryl has continued in the business as a successful independent publicist.

What acts do you work with?

I work with personalities for TV series, motion pictures, and special events. As far as music is concerned, I work with Kenny Rogers, Wayne Newton, Smothers Brothers, Mac Davis, and Cybil Shepherd, who is also working on an album right now. We also represent New Kids on the Block, Gloria Estefan, everyone from Gladys Knight to Henry Mancini to David Bowie to Tina Turner to Wayne Newton – who is now becoming a movie star. We have lots of different divisions within our company, so we handle motion pictures as well as performers and personalities on TV series.

How did you get started?

I majored in communications at Syracuse University and started as a tour guide with NBC. Then I was a secretary with a local news organization and from there I got into casting for five years at NBC. I got into production working on TV series for several years – still out of New York. I met Warren Cowan, who is the president of Rogers & Cowan, and he offered me a position with the company and brought me to Los Angeles. I have been with them for 10 years. I have been in the business for 18 years.

What does a publicist do?

You try to get the best exposure for your clients. There are very different campaigns. One is what I call "Nuts and Bolts," which is just typical interviews, articles, things that you read. Then there is the "creative campaign," which is coming up with the Hollywood stars, special tributes, awards, film retrospectives, tennis tournaments named after the client, and charity events. All of those things are important, too. You have to get to the entertainment community so that person becomes so hot their name is bandied about. You also have to get to the general public so they will buy records, watch the TV movies, or go out and see the films. Those are different campaigns that we put together.

Do you have a music background?

I really have an entertainment background that is very diversified. I have studied music, mass communications, and television production and I think it has all helped because each job has been very diversified.

Do you think it is necessary to have a college degree to do what you are doing?

I don't think so. I know that you have to start from the bottom and you have to pay your dues. I had to do that even with the four years of college education at Syracuse and summer school at UCLA. So I started as a tour guide. I came out of college thinking I was going to be a producer and I was shocked when I went to the employment bureau at NBC and they said, "Tour guide or secretary?" "But I'm a college graduate," I said. They said, "Tour guide or secretary?"

I think that the most important thing is practical experience. I think book knowledge is very important. In my business you must be able to type (I type all the time); you must be able to write (I have written bios, articles, items, all sorts of stories), and you have to be able to communicate (public address, oral interpretation, and all those courses are important because you have to speak with people). You have to get on the phone and convey whatever you are trying to say in 20 seconds to a very busy journalist. You've got to get to know these people and you've got to be professional and honest. Once you give them a story that is not true, they will never forgive you. That is very important. You put your reputation on the line when you deal with them.

What would you tell a young person who wants to get started in the business?

It is important to go after your goals. Write down your short-range goals. Where do you want to be in six months? a year? Then write your long-range goals. What would you like to be doing in five or 10 years? It's very important to get a position that is not a dead-end position, where there is growth, opportunity for movement, where you get a chance to meet other people.

You are your own salesperson; you have to sell yourself in the best way and you have to believe in yourself. If you don't believe in yourself, no one else will. Get to know the players. Read about the people in a particular company. Get to know who they are. Read publications about the business you're interested in – *Cashbox, Billboard, Hollywood Reporter*, or other trade papers. Volunteer for events of charities that deal with the record business. It is a good way to get to know people. Take classes and attend seminars.

What is important to remember is that the entertainment business is built on highs and lows. You can have a terrific day one day and a miserable day the next. It is not a normal type of job. You have to go with the flow, have a balance in your life where you work hard but you also play hard. Never forget that you have to have friends and family so you don't get so caught up in your job that you look around and it's July already.

The important thing to remember is that it is not a nine-to-five job. Very often you will be at the studios late at night or on photo sessions or you will have to attend events. When you attend an event you are not a guest, you are working. Your client depends on you; they are putting their career in your hands and you have got to do the best that you can because if something bad happens it is your responsibility. The most important thing is to get that positive press out there. You have got to pay your dues and you've just got to realize that it is not a regular job. You have to learn to deal with egos and lots of people. You must like people; that is very important.

<u>Resources</u>

ASCAP (American Society of Composers, Authors & Publishers)
One Lincoln Plaza
New York, NY 10023
212-595-3050
http://www.ascap.com

BMI (Broadcast Music Inc.)
320 West 57th Street
New York, NY 10019-3790
212-586-2000
http://www.bmi.com

SESAC (Headquarters)
55 Music Square East
Nashville, TN 37203
615-320-0055
http://www.sesac.com

Recommended Reading

The list below is a very small sampling of what is available in print. For periodicals, walk down to your local magazine stand and check out the music section. Most any book on the subject of music or the music business can be found at Amazon.com.

- *100 Careers in the Music Business* by Tanja L. Crouch
- *Career Opportunities in the Music Industry* by Shelly Field
- *The Music Business: Career Opportunities and Self-Defense* by Dick Weissman
- *How To Get a Job in the Music Industry* by Hatchek
- *This Business of Music* by Sidney Shemel and M. William Krasilvosky

- *Pollstar Magazine*
- *Mix Magazine*
- *Billboard Magazine*

ABOUT THE AUTHOR

Edgar Struble works in a wide range of media, with a focus in television and film. His career was launched in the mid-1970s from Nashville when he began a 15-year engagement as music director for Kenny Rogers. Since 1999, Edgar has been based in Los Angeles, where he's worked as music director and composer for such productions as the *Your Big Break* and *Greed* series and TV specials *Challenge of the Child Geniuses, It's Your Chance of a Lifetime,* and *The First Family's Holiday Gift to America* for FOX, as well as several documentary specials for TLC, A&E, and The History Channel. In association with Dick Clark Productions, he is music director and composer for the annual *Academy of Country Music Awards* and *American Music Awards* programs. He has released three CDs featuring country standards and his own compositions.

To learn more about Edgar and his work, visit www.edgarstruble.com.

Edgar Struble is available for music career seminars at high schools and colleges. For information, please contact Peter Panic Music, 17667 Sierra Hwy., Canyon Country, CA, 91351. Phone: 818-237-5167. Website: www.edgarstruble.com.

E-mail: edgar@edgarstruble.com

Breinigsville, PA USA
04 May 2010
237287BV00003B/1/P